ESSAYS ON BOND MARKET ECONOMICS

'Despite the status of bonds as "fixed income" assets, this book reminds investors to raise their shields for the uncanny in already unpredictable markets. Through a chronological account, Ray Choy offers pragmatic and unique perspectives to investment analysts and fund managers'.

Hanifah Hashim, Executive Director,
Franklin Templeton Investments

'Ray Choy's book provides an extensive coverage of topics on bond market economics. The essays not only challenge conventional wisdom on financial economics, but also provide answers to questions raised in the area with precision and clarity. These essays would be an extremely useful guide for students of financial economics.'

Arusha Cooray, Professor of Economics,
The University of Nottingham

'Ray Choy is a thought leader for the fixed income markets and its observers, and in this book, he has seamlessly managed to amalgamate standard economic theories with a practitioner's viewpoint, and has succinctly put forth a fresh perspective on the policy and market actions seen in a post-financial crisis world.'

Rahul Bajoria, Regional Economist,
Barclays Capital

ABOUT THE AUTHOR

The author, Swee Yew Choy, also known as Ray Choy, is presently the Director of Fixed Income & Currency Research at RHB Research Institute, a company of RHB Banking Group. He has been a financial markets practitioner since 2002, primarily in funds management and investment research, specialising in global macro asset allocation, fixed income and currencies. The author's diverse experience spans both Developed and Emerging Markets fixed income and currency macro strategy, bond funds management, equities investments, and credit ratings. The author is an award-winning analyst, ranked by The Asset, and has also received an award by Malaysia's Bond Pricing Agency in recognition of his team's contribution to the development of the bond market. He is a regular commentator on Bloomberg and other media channels, and is a frequently invited speaker at conferences across Asia.

Essays on Bond Market Economics

Ray S.Y. Choy

First published in this edition, 2016

ISBN-13: 978-1535326391

ISBN-10: 1535326395

Printed in the USA by CreateSpace, an Amazon.com company.

For family & friends

Contents

What is rational is real

and what is real is rational.

– G.W.F. Hegel

Prologue

Background

This book is a collection of essays written from December 2012 to December 2015, which were published pro bono in the periodical, The Edge Weekly (Malaysia), one of those exemplary cases of journalism which myself and many others in the financial markets and business community looked forward to reading. In fact, its attempts at objective, investigative and analytical journalism brought it both critical acclaim amongst its readers, as well as difficult moments, befitting of journalism which invokes its fair share of incisive critique.

It was towards this ethos of writing which I was challenged to present as naturally as would a financial markets practitioner and researcher, which I interpreted, perhaps to the dismay of some, with no qualms for the obfuscating presence of jargon and specialist terminology. After all, the periodical mainly targeted a niche market comprising of expert readers and professional investors.

An intended non-deterministic approach

A corollary of such a writing style is of course, the voluntary construction of multi-layered meanings and subtexts. This style would allow for different levels of interpretation and raise questions for further debate over norms of practice and theory within the subject of *bond market economics*, which is unique if considered as a distinctive nexus without *bonds* or *economics* having preponderance over the other. In fact, I remain a strong proponent that given the tilt of positivistic empirical practice of financial markets, a poststructuralist mental state needs to be placed in equally high regard; that is, without losing sight of discourse analysis and the critical re-evaluation of canonical impositions within the financial markets.

Against this ideology, one would surmise that language creates the financial markets and vice versa. This may be familiar to many, but my mentioning this brings to being hopes of emphasising the need for an open paradigm to the science and art of financial markets analysis. The construct of the language-ideas-financial markets interdependence cannot be better characterised by the relationship between central bank commentaries and its great influence on asset prices. At the other end of the spectrum, the media, both representing and influencing common and popular knowledge, is just as powerful, if not more powerful than central banks as formal institutions in rallying focal points of knowledge. These focal points in turn influence what the quantitatively-inclined term as volatility.

Consequently, it is important to reiterate that uncertainty is the name of the game in the financial markets if we were to take that aforementioned poststructuralist approach with its rejection of hegemonic dogma and comfortable structural canons.

Thus, this book attempts to circumvent a regurgitated bond market interpretation of linear models where multi-factor analysis helps to procure neat building blocks of risk-return components in providing analytical structure. This is not to suggest that pre-existing notions which provide this structure is insignificant, but rather, to provide a louder voice for minority ideas. The approach here is taken to extract subverted meanings and raise the profile of ideas which remain highly relevant yet often overlooked or eclipsed by some commonly accepted dogma. Hence, the essays here explain these subtexts and their use in practice and where relevant, can be seen as a critique of present-day paradigms.

Essay summaries

The first essay begins by articulating debt markets refinancing risk in controversial terms, as a Ponzi scheme. This scheme is possible, against the current period of easy monetary policy which has allowed for excess credit creation. Essentially, such schemes are organisations which require the replacement of capital and can be seen in various forms, from frequent corporate bond issuers' refinancing schemes and to the sceptic, even respected institutions such as pension funds.

The second essay focuses on components of sovereign debt analysis which in my opinion, have been sidelined by more popular narratives of certain key ratios, and the dominant status of quantitative methods of analysis.

The third essay, discusses the issue of declining bond yields which at the time of writing, had many worried over this being a structural and potentially permanent problem. From the September-1981 high of 15.8% for the 10-year US Treasury, the flagship bond market, we have since seen a consistent decline in yields, currently returning sparsely above a paltry 1%. Institutional reasons are discussed as a major driver of this yield trend.

The fourth essay, an affront to the frequently criticised basic form of the Efficient Markets Hypothesis, draws a distinction between markets which can be more efficient than another, in terms of more accurately pricing and representing market sentiment. Furthermore, the idea that risks and its impact, although stemming from the same source, has differential impacts on different market spaces, challenges universalist views of risk. Risks cannot be simply expressed as sigma, a psychological and representational misnomer, even if it arises from a common platform.

The fifth essay continues on the idea that some markets, such as the large and liquid US Treasuries market, are more efficient than others and is therefore a good source of information. This again requires, a nuanced interpretation of the Efficient Markets Hypothesis. This essay also revisits the incorporation of macroeconomic information in this market, and hence a more conventional viewpoint of understanding the bond market is utilised as compared to the structure-institutions perspective of the third essay.

The sixth essay develops an additional approach to pricing information, the behavioural approach, one which has been increasingly discussed at the present decade with the rising relevance of information economics and behavioural finance, an additional angle to the traditional macroeconomic variables and institutional factors approaches as exemplified in the preceding essays.

The introduction of the seventh essay discusses the ethical purpose of the financial markets as opposed to its utilitarian form. Though reductionist in its approach, it conceives of the gamblers' mindset towards financial markets as part of the problem of unreasonable risk-taking despite having to scrape the barrel for returns.

The eighth essay explains the experience of how central bank and other forms of focused authoritative communications impact financial markets, highlighting the importance of language and discourse analysis by the financial markets, a community which is often easily mistaken as one which is paradigmatically scientific and quantitative.

The ninth essay considers constructive ambiguity in a financial world which frequently demands transparency of information, and that could be at times a misguided totalitarian belief. As with any trade-off, transparency has its advantage, although it often comes at a cost.

The tenth essay objectively weighs the idea of whether innovations in monetary policy, namely quantitative easing, should be viewed with suspicion. It is an obvious notion to declare that economic histories are never identical; hence, innovations in policy are borne out of the constraints of a specific context and can only be judged retrospectively.

The eleventh essay calls into question the proposition of the US as a unipolar economic and political power. The ongoing debate has been rife that the US is losing its grip as a supranational, and this appeared to fulfil the popular idea of "The Rise of the East and The Fall of The West". This was also a period in which the US and the other hegemonic powers of the developed world appeared to be expending far too much political capital. This event serves notice that one must always prepare for the unexpected, and that hegemons and their influence are not static givens.

The twelfth essay suggests that political risk events tend to be centred on a country, limiting the transmission mechanism of positive or negative effects on the markets. This could partly be due to the fact that markets respond in a short-term manner, compared to political effects which tend to be long drawn. At the point of writing this introduction, a few weeks have passed since the Brexit vote on the UK's EU Referendum on 23rd June 2016, and up to this point the financial markets have corroborated my intuitive hypothesis that such political risk events tend to lead to limited, non-contagious financial markets damage.

The obsession with central bank rhetoric is emphasised in the thirteenth essay, and again, marks the extent of institutional influence regardless of how present anti-establishment sentiment may be opined as arbitrary or ranted against. The nature of central banking as a social construct remains significantly pertinent and oftentimes, requires financial market practitioners to intuit as an artist rather than analyse as a scientist.

The fourteenth essay suggests that the appreciation of risk at the individual level is relative and asymmetrical, hence the degree to which risk is relevant, discerned, differentiated and acted upon is also a case of information being viewed similarly and therefore, having the same degree of perceived utility across different individuals. The purpose of this explanation aims to question whether there is a common understanding of risk and emphasise inherent difficulties in its definition.

The fifteenth essay supports the case that public sector finance such as taxation policy should play a greater role and should be provided greater significance in the discourse of sovereign credit analysis. It is argued that public sector financial analysis within sovereign credit analysis lends greater insight into the mechanics of government cash flow sustainability, and that we need to differentiate government or sovereign debt analysis from general economic analysis.

The sixteenth essay hypothesises that the directionality or the lack of it in a market, depends on whether reality and expectations or sentiment are congruent with each other. Thus, being overly confident of an imagined reality can exacerbate volatility, particularly one recognised by an authority such as the central bank. This essay also characterises the carry trade as arbitrage between both financial assets and real assets, beyond the traditional notion of arbitrage on yields and interest rates, an effect of persistently accommodative monetary policy.

The seventeenth essay revisits the extreme view held at that time by investors on the commodity exporters which had been grouped as a class of high-risk investments with the emerging markets. An attempt was made to attenuate extreme views on the cliché of the "resource-cursed" economies. Likening this to the earlier mentioned poststructuralist mental state, this is a question of whether an imposed narrative had been manipulated towards for an intended type of financial market action.

The eighteenth essay was authored at the end of 2014, an annual summary of my views on the fixed income and currency outlook for the next year. The recurrent issue of central bank policy had arisen due to worries of a withdrawal of easy monetary policy (which I opine will frequently prove misplaced, as it did at the time of writing in June 2016), alongside the discourse over the differentiation between emerging markets' and developing markets' risk profiles. Despite the oft-quoted "flat world" hypothesis, economic and financial geographies remain important in structuring financial market thinking.

The nineteenth essay's title though seemingly unintuitive, underscores that the market's persistent uncertainties are positive for the safe haven trade, thus increasing the value of the haven or "risk-free" security, and at the time of writing, was benchmarked by US Treasuries. Therefore, while bonds which possess credit risk could be negatively buffeted by uncertainties, some of its returns would have been positively influenced by the fact that its overall yield is also, in part, tied to the "risk-free" rate. Finally, this essay argues that the credit spread need not always be largely a function of "credit risk", but some other imputation of perceived risk.

The twentieth essay expounds on the epistemology of sovereign credit ratings. On one hand, a quantitative science is sometimes both applied and expected by authors and users of these ratings while on the other hand, their authoritative methodology papers suggest a more balanced approach with little evidence of bias. As with various forms of media, readers need to sometimes discern between objective and subjective reports, and whether a specific intellectual agenda is being advanced at the expense of a more balanced reading.

The twenty-first essay, explicitly discusses central bank decisions and bond yields in the context of game theory, which can be particularly useful when analysing relative values of the bonds of major markets. It can be mundane to consistently consider central bank policy decisions as a function of traditional macroeconomic variables such as growth, inflation, and employment.

A repositioning from macro issues to micro-level issues is discussed in the twenty-second essay, emphasising that the microeconomics of bond transactions play a special role in bond valuations. Liquidity can be viewed from both a top-down and bottom-up approach.

The final essay of this book, the twenty-third essay, is the second essay in this compilation which focuses on the markets outlook for the following year, then, the outlook for 2016. A more subdued view of the global economy has subsequently developed, fuelling better bidders on the safe haven sovereign bond markets with reserve currency status, in particular, the US Treasuries. Additionally, the outlook was written at a time when economic growth and monetary policy divergence between the global economies emerged as the base case expectation for 2016, reflecting the improving economic strength of the US economy. However, one could question whether the US Treasuries should have performed as well as they did, since the US economy had a stronger outlook compared with its peers of the advanced economies league, which were at the time in the doldrums. Again, this is one area which theory and actual market movements need further reconciliation and explanation. The pessimistic tone of this essay, with the sub-headings of "Climbing Out of a Well" and "Giving Credence to Pessimism" would later prove to have materialised by mid-2016, as the global economy appears to have remained addicted to easy monetary policy, quantitative easing, and continued threats to global hegemonic institutional arrangements, including the rise of anti-establishment sentiment.

Context

Firstly, some of these essays were market commentaries pertaining to specific time periods, and have been placed in chronological order. Being written for an expert audience, there was a paucity of definitions and studious explanations; as such, there was a need to provide useful summaries, as italicised, at the beginning of each essay in order to distill a general concept or hypothesis which the essay had functionalised or alluded to.

Secondly, this book provides a narrative of the events of the bond markets from my personal and limited perspective as one who is deeply involved in the financial markets and therefore influenced by a certain mode of thinking and written expression.

Thirdly, these essays are an artefact of a short history, with a focus on the bond markets from the end of 2012 to the end of 2015, and notably, was written towards the maturing stage of a choppy economic cycle in light of the frequently considered debate that the next economic crisis could occur very soon in 2017, assuming a simplistic and crudely-conceived pattern repeat since the recent major crises of 1997/98 and 2007/08.

Furthermore, the essays were constrained by a word limit which respects the requirements of the publishing periodical, which in fact, was very useful in managing my time and preventing my ramblings from going overboard. Both unfortunately and fortunately, the limited exposition meant that there was a need for greater effort at interpretation and analysis by the reader.

Finally, while effort had been made to provide persisting and normative theoretical insights, market commentaries limited to the short-term context, were included as was expected for practical reasons of periodic writing and for readers from the financial markets who had to procure functional insights.

Prologue

In context of the subdued stage of the global economy in which this book was written, it is perhaps possible that readers comprehend my frequent use of the words "uncertainty" and "volatility". Having experienced the 2007/08 Great Financial Crisis, financial market practitioners such as I remain suspicious of the pie in the sky. In particular, bond market personnel tend to be viewed as a pessimistic lot, but as an ex-boss used to say, this is an inevitable trait of perceptive financial market analysts.

Essay 1

December 2012

The Debt Ponzi

A Ponzi scheme occurs when new investments or cash flows from new investors are used to pay off old investments. This is usually constructed for the purpose of repaying the promise of an unusually high investment return.

In the debt markets, refinancing schemes might be considered a euphemism for a Ponzi scheme, although its legitimacy appears superficially well-founded which unfortunately, provides a return which is often not commensurate with risks underwritten.

Also, the credit creation cycle has been known to be self-reinforcing and potentially risky, at some point in time. Nonetheless, capital market participants need to be aware of this inevitability and at a minimum, attempt to deal with the risky cycle of constant debt refinancing.

Hence, it would be natural to assess whether an entity is expected to have a sufficiently long lifespan with ongoing cash flows or value creation which accords it an economically legitimate right to refinance constantly. Additionally, it is worth questioning, on a regular basis and implemented as part of credit assessment methodology, the track record and frequency of refinancing that an entity had and is likely to have the intention to engage in.

~

Debt crises are often almost inevitable and self-reinforcing. Whenever a deep economic slowdown or recession occurs, systemic risks come knocking at the door. Such problems can often be first seen when NPLs (non-performing loans) begin to rise, and banks attempt to desperately grow their asset base to publish an NPL ratio which appears artificially healthier due to a larger denominator. Resultantly, banks engage in a mathematical ploy. However, this can be difficult to detect, particularly when a rising asset base is often associated with business success and economic prosperity. Try telling a bank manager to stop lending when everyone else is. Hence, the incentives are not aligned toward a comprehensive view of risks, particularly when performance measures are geared towards a myopic view of topline revenues.

A subsequent effect of seemingly lower NPL ratios is the perceived capability to lend further. Apart from the optics of healthier bank financial ratios, there is also the self-delusion of successful risk management, impenetrable credit quality and overconfidence. Furthermore, indebted companies which repay loans via more loans helps maintain a façade of debt servicing ability. Cash levels and flows appear higher as financing is injected. Due to a self-reinforcing loop, the problem itself becomes more difficult to control, being a loop which expands further outward, involving ever greater numbers of individuals, banks, corporations and governments.

After all, the time to potential default is probably more than a loan officer's career lifespan with a single bank. Hence, it is of little personal benefit to pursue deepening credit risks which in itself could cause an actual default as lines of liquidity are withdrawn. Furthermore, the harbinger of doom tends to be unpopular. The bad news can always be delayed, or at least, for as long as the debt is being serviced through fresh financing.

Due to the vested interest of banks to lend more and obtain short-term rewards, both lending and borrowing are encouraged. This is particularly in this age of easy monetary policy, triggered by the last major financial crisis of 2007/08. With most developed economies pricing money at near-free rates, banks and similar economic agents themselves are borrowing and lending at negligible cost. However, due to today's very liquid and open financial markets, monies which were meant for ailing economies (i.e. developed markets in general) are being lent to growth economies and sectors (i.e. developing markets in general). While low interest rates are meant to provide a countercyclical push against slowing growth, the nature of risk management in the private sector is directly opposed to lending to the less fortunate entities. Risk management parameters require a limit to lending for companies and governments with poorly performing ex-post financial ratios.

The problem is exacerbated given the increasing liberalisation of financial markets which raises the extent of cross-linkages in the flow of international money. Hence, money can easily flow to entities which do not need it, and exit entities which need it. This gives rise to disastrous chemistry. Then, the contractionary loop is increasingly self-reinforced, taking away the umbrella during rainy weather. Financially healthy entities then, risk becoming bloated with excess credit, which leads to spendthrift behaviour and investments in risky and probably uneconomic projects.

Risky and uneconomic projects are again, a matter of relatives and which stage of the economic cycle one is in. Understanding this through the cycle and the flow of time is very important.

To explain, let us think about an example. When borrowing rates are 2%, does that not make a return on investment (ROI) of 3% economic? If this were the case, company X would like to borrow at 2%. Company X also borrows based on the market's preferred duration, say, 5 years. As time goes on and risk aversion sets in during an economic downturn, yields or borrowing rates rise. However, the project which Company X invested in has yet to complete. Perhaps there was a variation order in the contract, or in the case of governments, politicians needed more money to win an election. However, the market is now willing to lend for only 3 years at 3%. As such, the project's ROI of 3% now covers the cost of financing. Therefore, what was once profitable at 3%

has become a lot less attractive through the passage of time.

Assuming borrowers expect this to occur, then, would there not be an incentive to borrow more when rates are low? In other words, would it not be better to borrow counter-cyclically? Unfortunately, borrowing is based on the availability and value of collateral, the availability of expected cash flows from an investment, and the availability of investment projects. It is difficult to explain to both borrowers and lenders of capital that the borrowing decision is largely based on the decision of timing capital costs. There is also a great limit in the ability to foresee the capital raising decision through the business cycle.

Apart from the difficulty of counter-cyclical credit creation, lending activity has the tendency to be pro-cyclical, where in times of economic prosperity, required rates of return on investments are low due to higher risk appetite and confidence. On the other hand, expected returns could rise unreasonably when capital flight occurs alongside diminished confidence.

The difference perhaps, between a Ponzi scheme and the risk of a potential debt bubble is the fact that fraud is not involved, since borrowers and investors are willing, while the Ponzi scheme offers the promise of higher returns.

Hence, ironically, it seems that a Ponzi scheme can be considered more attractive with the prospect and promise of higher returns, which may actually materialise for forerunners. To compare this to the debt market, it is akin to being the first bond investor with a put option to the secondary market before an unending series of refinancing schemes, maturity extensions and debt expansions.

The property sectors in Europe and the US during the 2007/08 Crisis were particularly affected by this problem, since a greater supply of financing meant higher property prices, which in turn led to the need for more financing. In a story that we are all very familiar with now, at some point in time, governments needed to bear the burden, leading to an eventual loss of confidence in government-issued debt.

However, some governments have appeared to handle the growing debt Ponzi better than others. Following the 2007/08 Crisis, Europe was blamed for a weak institutional structure to help govern debt issuances and usage, and yet less developed countries with a shorter track record of debt management are experiencing ever-compressing yields. Is this simply a case of excess liquidity chasing a limited pool of investments? Otherwise, are there fundamentally sound reasons for such monies being invested in emerging market opportunities?

Sometimes, such arguments and debates are simply capricious and it may be difficult to draw comfort or conclusion from opinions based on a limited dataset, or from information that is neither robustly inductive nor safely deductive. Once upon a time, the institutional structure and governance of Europe and US were lauded as being supportive of the flow of financing throughout the economy, integral to matching savings with investments. Trusted central banks were the epicentre of low bond yields, enhancing the flow of credit to the economy. In fact, high debt ratios were generally and variously ignored. There was once I read an article highlighting the problems of a misled governance structure as underpinning the European debt crisis. Thus, does that suggest that many less developed countries are actually more highly capable of governance than their European, US and Japanese counterparts?

While it is true that institutional structures could play a role in determining the success of a monetary union and its debt programmes, there is little evidence that the theory behind an "ideal" monetary union could yield optimal results. The theory surrounding monetary unions has not had sufficient track record or substantive evidence to propose the best possible structure. In fact, the world might want to thank Europe for taking on this highly difficult and dangerous experiment for generations of governments to learn from. Even so, the experiment remains ongoing, and what we know is largely normative.

While Europe continues to take the blame for playing with fire and entangled in a debt crisis, most of the world has forgotten that debt crises are indeed self-reinforcing and inevitably cyclical. When the cost of debt declines, it is difficult, whether psychologically or via market pressures, to avoid the temptation to expand aggressively.

Amid these problems, the world continues to refine its experimentation with monetary unions, innovative financing structures, and psychological gaming between central banks and markets. Thus, I believe that political bickering and solving problems at the macro-institutional level are not enough. Regulation needs to understand the link between sovereign and banking crises, and the difficulty of delinking that risk. While the latter has often been discussed as a solution, I suppose a better approach would be in understanding and managing that risk, rather than running counter against the inevitable.

Risk management practices at an operational level need to be examined closely, alongside macroprudential measures such as higher capital requirements which attempt to limit the unreasonable expansion of lending activity. Of course, this has been addressed via Basel Committee measures, although this considers issues at the macro level, and the dissemination and execution of this rest largely with the operational level. Hence, whether the principles of risk management are inculcated at the operational level would require a significant investment in resources to align incentives correctly, such as the use of risk-adjusted returns rather than sales as performance objectives.

About this, the substance of effect needs to supersede the shape and form of policies and procedures. However, these regulations on lending activity cannot be contradicted by low interest rates for too long. Eventually, central banks will need to take the responsibility of raising rates gently, or conduct a form of monetary policy normalisation to that effect. This is indeed both a macroeconomic and moral responsibility to the citizenry, since excessively low interest rates for too long can be distortive to utility allocation and cause a build-up of asset price bubbles. More worrying, would be the behavioural impact that low rates of return on the debt markets cause, and the accompanying cycle of higher borrowing and uneconomic investments.

Ultimately, it remains to be seen whether new regulations and the rationalisation towards smaller trading books and tighter leashes will help. While this is all very much hopeful, it is necessary that governments and regulators are not merely responding to a political and regulatory cycle, which has become all too apparent during periods of crises and government change.

Essay 2

January 2013

Appraising Sovereign Creditworthiness

Macroeconomic metrics are often used as an important guideline to assessing the creditworthiness of a sovereign debt issuer. However, this is exactly what it is – a guideline, not an absolute decree.

Also, an excessive reference to commonly used macroeconomic metrics such as the debt-to-GDP ratio, fiscal deficit-to- GDP ratio, current account balance-to-GDP ratio, GDP growth rate, GDP per capita and inflation rate could detract from issues which pertain to the effective management of a nation's economy and public finances.

In this regard, it is important to remember that sovereign credit analysis as a concept should not be excessively separated from the topic of public financial management. In fact, the conceptual analysis of public finances can lend a more involved insight into the repayment capabilities of a government. Furthermore, ex-post debt levels provide little information over the utilisation of finances and future cash flows from the government; this must then be compared to government investments, such as those via parastatals, versus current revenues and expenditures.

The philosophy of investing in a government bond, therefore, requires a firmer link to the philosophy of qualitative and financial credit analysis. Through this viewpoint, sovereign credit analysis would not be as esoteric and vague as perceived.

While there is much to be explored, this essay focuses on aspects related to interpreting issues of sovereign credit analysis, beyond conventional macroeconomic metrics, such as contingent liabilities, sources of tax revenues and the role of foreign holdings in the bond markets.

~

A commonly used measure of a government's creditworthiness is reflected in the debt-to-GDP ratio, and this may have gained greater popularity ever since the debt debacles in the peripheral European countries flared up during the Financial Crisis of 2007/8. However, a ratio in itself does not tell us much. For example, on aggregate, Eurozone debt was estimated at 90% of GDP in 2012 while the debt in Japan was forecasted at about 220%. However, the Yen was, for most of 2012, considered a safe haven currency and similarly, yields on the Japanese government bonds hardly budged despite the negative sovereign rating action on Japan in 2012. This was very much similar to the US case, where yields trended down following the historic downgrade by Standard & Poor's in August 2011.

In Japan, a large stock of savings overseas is said to have helped prevent currency and bond market panic, while the US used its strategic advantage of reserve currency status to benefit from global financial repression with impunity. Nonetheless, identifying and understanding the scope of Japan's stash of overseas assets, as well as determining how long the US would hold its strategic financial market advantage are questions that remain difficult to answer.

In Malaysia, industry peers have often raised concerns over the rising level of debt in this country (forecasted to remain slightly below 55% of GDP in 2013), and the narrow range of revenues supporting it. This brings us to a rhetorical question – what does it mean for a major commodity exporter to diversify sources of tax revenues? Additionally, in the event oil exports decline over time, being an expendable resource, does that not mean that an automatic diversification of potential tax revenues would occur? When oil revenues and sector activity drop, does that mean that the economic base shifts away from the primary to tertiary sector, which subsequently causes a diversification of the tax base? That said, recent evidence suggests great strides in Malaysia's private sector growth, alongside robust consumption expenditure and tourism receipts. Also, the tendency, over time, for developing economies to increase the tax base derived from indirect taxes such as value-added taxes and goods and services taxes lends further credence to public sector finances.

However, the answer as to whether the economy is able to draw on a diversified range of tax sources is not simple. On one hand, where a commodity exporter has been naturally endowed with resources, it may not be reasonable to expect the economy to derive a bulk of taxes from the non-commodities sectors. In this case, the benefit of natural resource endowment suggests an element whereby both the economic cycle and tax collections would experience customary volatility. Additionally, the expectation of diversification results in a trade-off to economic specialisation, and this may not be optimal to the economy and trade partners.

It is also questionable if apparently volatile commodities revenues such as that from oil would automatically extrapolate to volatilities in government revenues. Given an expanding middle class in developing economies and a hectic phase of emerging markets' infrastructure development, it is more likely for commodities prices to have an upside skew. Empirical evidence suggests that oil prices have a greater tendency for an upside surprise, due to factors such as geological and geopolitical mishaps, alongside collective supply control on top of a commodity that is generally demand-inelastic. Simple volatility combined with an expectation of mean reversion cannot be equivalent to volatility with a price-favourable probability distribution, that is, a favourable skew towards higher prices.

Another important inquiry for consideration is the nature of contingent liabilities, and this has often been discussed in Malaysia, following the rise of private-public sector partnerships for major infrastructure projects. Government-guaranteed debt has in fact been increasing, and so have the papers sold by issuers with strong government links.

Besides being a confusing taxonomical issue, I believe that the general nomenclature has lost sight of the importance of the financial sector in computing contingent liabilities – in order to compute contingent liabilities, it is often misinterpreted as largely computable off-balance sheet debt. Contingent liabilities must also take into account the expected value of risks crystallising from financial sector distress. Therefore, the comprehensive assessment of contingent liabilities comprises the assessment of both government-supported debts as well as the probability of risks materialising from the financial system, which governments and taxpayers would have to bear, whether voluntarily or involuntarily.

Noting this for our example of Malaysia, it is worth mentioning that Malaysia's financial system has made great advances via macroprudential measures, reflecting in low inflation rates, stability in GDP growth, low unemployment rates, declining NPL ratios, manageable credit growth, and prudent provisioning standards. Sufficient account needs to be made of reduced contingent liability risks from Malaysia's financial system.

A method to assess foreign investor confidence is to examine the size of their holdings in the bond market. Again, the interpretation of this can be flawed in a few ways. Firstly, a significant size of foreign holdings in the bond market is not necessarily negative, and could, in fact, indicate strong investor confidence in an economy. To assess this factor, it would be better to evaluate the inflows of funds, its persistence, and the size of outflows when it occurs. The point on persistence is particularly important, especially when observed over a period of several years, since it could indicate a long-term, structural shift in the economy or investment policies by investors, and such shifts tend to be less volatile than the headlines of short-term capital flows.

Also, if outflows are minimal in a given month, as compared to the overall size of the bond market, there should be mitigated concerns that the risk of capital flight would result in a major crisis in the cost of financing. While this is retrospective, the important takeaway is to evaluate the depth of the market, its ability to absorb capital flows, and remain functional in the event capital flows actually occur, as they always do.

Furthermore, having a high degree of foreign holdings are useful in maintaining public finance discipline and ensuring capital account convertibility. What foreign holdings essentially provide is a feedback mechanism through the capital market as an international watchdog.

While caution should not be thrown to the wind, we ought to think thrice before declaring a high amount of foreign ownership in the bond market as a negative risk.

By providing the link to the external economies, the capital markets are an important facilitator in internationalising and liberalising an economy. All in all, constructive criticisms that global investors level at a country should be appreciated. Without international feedback, there would be no impetus to work towards economic progress, fiscal consolidation, and toward achieving a higher sovereign credit rating.

Essay 3

February 2013

Falling Return Expectations on Bonds

The traditional view of bond yields is usually constructed through the building blocks of risk premia. Broadly, this would include policy interest rates, credit risk premiums and liquidity risks. However, the idea of structural changes can be difficult to pinpoint, which has led to the continuing conundrum of low yields, challenging traditional risk premium and term structure models.

For practitioners, this means that traditional yield trends and models may have very little relevance for forecasting purposes. This is understandable since the conundrum of low yields in recent years has been driven by a mix of both central bank perceptions as well as institutional changes post-Bretton Woods.

Part of the reason for low yields are linked to the attitudes toward central bank independence versus coordination with fiscal authorities, and the macro trends towards higher debt levels accompanied by a greater degree of central planning, government power and the blurred delineation between private and public sectors. Inflation and financial stability targets may at times conflict with expansionary goals at Ministries of Finance; hence a degree of coordination may be warranted and inevitable.

Furthermore, the existence of a reserve currency post-Bretton Woods would provide the United States (US) significant power in determining the cost of financing in their domestic currency. The dissolution of the Gold peg during President Nixon's era allowed for a rapid repricing of expected returns and hence, bond yields. Today, the stability of international financial arrangements and monopolisation of the risk-free rate via US Treasuries and its reserve currency status has led to the low yield volatility environment, at least until there is a change in the post-Bretton Woods global financial architecture.

The reasons for low yields and financial repression are vast and varied. Hence, the limited scope of this essay serves to provide a brief overview of the low yield conundrum and how some market participants are reacting to this situation.

~

Despite the decline in bond yields, assumptions about long-term expected returns are still based on outdated historical data. Historical nominal bond returns in the major economies of the US, UK, and Germany averaged circa 4.5% over the last century. Today, average yields in these economies struggle to exceed 2.5%. Bond returns and yields are also declining in developing countries, due to the influx of portfolio capital flows. In fact, even high yield bonds are benefiting from a liquidity-driven rally compressing high grade-to-high yield spreads, suggesting diminishing discernment on credit risks in the fervent hunt for yield.

In view of current trend lines, future bond returns are more likely to stoop under half of the long-term historical average. However, despite these facts, the optimism of a stronger economy and rising inflation in the future has led to a complacency where mean reversion to long-term historical returns are hoped for.

Simplistic reasons for this long-term mean reversion to higher bond yields include the upward skew to commodity prices which can cause higher inflation, and the general belief that total factor productivity and global GDP growth are on a trend rise given technological improvements, advances in the knowledge economy, and globalisation.

On a more cynical note, the high return expectations are perhaps more of a justification rather than a logical rationale, due to: 1) a misguided belief of status quo bond returns to comfort anchoring biases; and 2) the difficulty of procuring acceptance by investment committees and actuaries to internalise normative explanations of a low return world, made more difficult when referenced to the familiar comfort of historical statistics.

However, the real financial market as it stands, defies historical statistics of higher returns for bonds, and does not explain why inflation-adjusted returns are struggling to provide a return above zero. As such, rational macroeconomic expectations are finding it more difficult to explain such low bond returns. While short-term yield curve slope changes have empirically proven to indicate the direction of economic growth about a year in advance, disappearing risk premiums and flattening term premiums over the long-term have not been particularly well-explained.

The economic rationale for the fall in bond returns are numerously suggested, and have gained greater interest given the swathe of crises we had to contend with over the last half of a decade. A poor return outlook in recent times, exacerbated by uncertainties over the quicksand of global politics and fiscal risks, will likely keep bond returns low.

While it is difficult to quantify, changes in global politics and the distrust over capitalism will likely have a secular impact over investing behaviour. Should capitalist ideals lose headway to collectivist philosophy with government economic control and taxes rising, the confidence and motivation for the private sector's compass of profit-orientation could cause wants and needs on risk-return levels to decline. Already, the rise in savings ratios coupled with ongoing deleveraging in the Anglo-Saxon economies, the yardsticks of capitalism, are signs of such winds of change. Safe haven bond markets performed tremendously well following the 2007/08 Crisis until today (mid-2014), and negative yields were not just one-off events, but spanned over several months. This negative yield scenario was a function where capital protection requirements superseded return requirements.

Economic policy innovations, meanwhile, bring markets through the frontier of zero interest rate policy, pressuring down return expectations. Concomitantly, this could erode expected risky asset returns, since these returns were perceived to be relatively good in the context of suppressed bond returns.

In relation to this, a self-reinforcing cycle may have already been created, where lower risk-free rates reduce risky asset risk premiums, which in turn drag down risk-free rates since such lower returns appear progressively and relatively more acceptable on an ex-post basis.

Secular issues aside, the drop in bond returns need to be practically addressed in the medium-term, as a pensioner may need to expect lower returns going forward. Funds which provide for long-term insurance and pension liabilities may need to reserve for a gap between payouts and actual cash flows, which may become wider-than-expected if return requirements remain fixated on the high side.

Governments, government-linked funds, and pension funds will need to consider if promised or statutory return requirements need to be revised downwards. Meanwhile, non-tax-exempt private investors may face a more difficult time since tax rates are more likely to remain unchanged or even higher as global fiscal deficits rise, and this is a serious predicament when applied to already thinning portfolio returns.

The risk of not revising down long-term expected return assumptions is that excessive risk-taking occurs to make up for the gap in required payouts. Many pension funds in Europe are likely to have difficulties paying up future liabilities following several years of weak equity market returns and post-crisis bond yields. Consequently, either a higher portfolio risk profile or broken promises will have to follow the return gap. Expectations need to be managed, and it would be highly misrepresentative to frame future returns on historical returns.

In addition, it is also important for investors and those marketing to investors that a change in mentality on returns is needed. Future cash flow planning is required in the context of very low returns from a fixed-income investment portfolio. Insurance premiums and savings plans may also need to be constructed to rise over time to provide for a given level of protection and expected income. In connection, beating inflation via bonds may be more difficult than initially expected, if possible at all. Capital preservation on the bond portfolio rather than returns to fund a retirement need to be prioritised, given the subdued outlook for future total returns.

Essay 4

March 2013

Of Cyprus & Systemic Risks

Bank runs and systemic risks are correlated with each other, which makes the issue of deposit haircuts particularly sensitive. It can lead to a denting of confidence, leading greater implications with regards to sovereign credit risk and the sustainability of the banking system.

There are several ways of analysing whether deposit haircuts are a major form of potential systemic risk. One is somewhat less universal, and requires the existence of a liquid and actively traded sovereign bond market, and price movements here are useful indicators to gauge if panic has set in. This is what makes the currency market particularly more relevant and important for assessing market reactions, and also helps detect whether a particular risk has spread beyond localisation.

With this thought, it is important that risk is classified as general, or is in the process of morphing into one that affects a broader range of asset classes and the real economy.

An interesting idea is whether the information regarding a malignant risk is expected, and the extent to which these expectations have had time to diffuse through the capital markets. Usually, risks are discussed in terms of their surprise factor, but the extent of a surprise is dependent on both an ageing and diffusion of the information, which can ironically be helped by transmission delays.

However, the equitable treatment of investors and the public, alongside issues of misinformation (such as the "sheepskin" effect) remains a distinctly important issue for the purpose of faith and trust in the marketplace, which again, can be assessed as a form of surprise, which is an asset pricing issue assuming it is noticed amid the complex policy bureaucracy. The case of Cyprus is a classic example of the problem of reneging and policy inconsistency.

~

The proposed haircut to deposits at Cyprus, or more euphemistically, "tax levy", warrants some analysis with regards to the fear of this event evolving into a system-wide shock, and its implications for bond market investors and economists. While the nature of analysis may appear ex-post, a discussion of this event is important since it gives input with regards to the appropriate investment response for the current event, and identifies common patterns for such events that may re-occur given the evolving nature of the Eurozone debt crisis. An analysis of this event would also prepare us to cope better with a recurrence of such risks, and to differentiate between the proposed Cyprus deposit haircut with broader versions of systemic risk events.

Systemic versus localised risk

The proposed deposit haircut needs to be first defined as to whether it constitutes systemic or localised risk. Having occurred, the market has defined this risk as localised on account of the following facts: 1) there was no evidence of an accelerated rise in related yields of the heavily indebted "peripheral" countries Italy and Spain, despite the current spotlight on their political instability and structural economic cracks, and 10-year bond yields in these nations are still more than 100 basis points below their 1-year high; 2) conversely, Cyprus government bonds were singled-out and heavily sold, rising 100 basis points on its 2020 maturity. What these respectively suggest are: 1) this is not a systemic risk event, which is again, seen from the very mild reaction of the broader Euro bonds market; and 2) the risk is localised.

What makes the Cyprus event more contained than systemic has much to do with the pricing in of anticipated versus unanticipated information. This event, in credit rating terms, was not particularly shocking, since 2 of the 3 international rating agencies had already rated Cyprus as CCC, which are past two non-investment grade rating bands (i.e. BB and B) below the BBB investment grade category. All 3 major rating agencies classify Cyprus as non-investment grade, implying a high probability of default. This point is important since the centrality of risk lies within the link between the sovereign and banking system. To interpret the credit ratings, the banking system in Cyprus was already economically insolvent. Its existence has been kept afloat by the central bank's excess liquidity policy, allowing EU regulators to delay a worsening of the EU economic crisis. This suggests that the fundamental problems remain unresolved up to this day, in view of continued output gaps today and political instabilities in the Eurozone.

Another reason for the localization of the risk is the paradoxical situation where, due to the protraction of the problems in Cyprus and the lack of prompt reforms by regulators, a wide distribution of information regarding the problems in Cyprus has already allowed bond market prices to adjust closer to equilibrium whereby economic insolvency is being priced in. The equilibrium setting of the market has also been helped by the fact that Cyprus is a relatively small economy, and therefore, the re-pricing of Cypriot-linked assets on existing balance sheets and portfolios will have little clout in terms of domino risk effects.

Structural investment implications

For bond investors, what this implies is a paradox where high grade securities could be riskier since this is where complacency clusters. Complacency leads to information asymmetries, which bear the risk of potential adverse amplification should a negative asset re-pricing flare up.

The greater the "sheepskin" effect (such as in AAA CDOs during the US subprime credit crisis), the greater the risk of information asymmetry and volatile investment returns.

Consequently, it is worth considering high yield securities which few have confidence in, given that the negativity had already been imputed to prices. While the last statement is somewhat obvious, it is important to connect this idea to two links: 1) unanticipated default risks have a greater impact on investor outperformance or underperformance versus the market; and 2) the degree of anticipation is correlated with the time-seasoning of default risk information, and the extent to which the information is widely distributed. In relation to information distribution, the economic insolvency of the sovereign and banks in Cyprus was already known as indicated by credit ratings. Furthermore, the time-seasoning of information which aids in the distribution process was ironically helped by the lag of a regulatory solution. Consequently, whichever off-equilibrium valuation reaction occurs on and following the Cyprus event is more likely to be behavioural and therefore, transient.

Regulatory credibility

To conclude, caution needs to be highlighted with regards to the regulatory approach to the bailout of financial institutions. Firstly, it is interesting to note that in the Cyprus proposal, deposits of below €100,000 would be subject to the haircut, despite eligibility for deposit insurance. The comfort of a deposit insurance scheme and the consistency of policies are what prevent bank runs from occurring, since bank runs depend on the perception of individuals, how they influence each other and the coordination of their withdrawals. Perhaps there was a reason for regulators to propose the tax? Is the regulator itself tainted with moral hazard by letting depositors share the burden given the debilitated banking system of a small economy? Or more constructively, is the regulator sending out a signal that it is aware of the imbalances in the Cypriot banking system and the potentially unruly nature of activities therein?

Due to the proposal of this "unique" tax levy on deposits by the EU, financial institutions and politicians may now have more reason to self-regulate. Nonetheless, it could be now more difficult for market participants to fulfil their side of the implicit contract of having full faith in the intentions of policymakers and the credibility and consistency of EU financial system policies.

Essay 5

April 2013

What Bond Yields are Saying (Part 1)

The size of the US Treasuries market creates a very important reference point as information, thoughts and concepts coalesce with trading behaviour. An idea that is often debated is whether bond yields are currently too low. The common answer to this is "yes", given the existing framework of existing yield levels. Traditional theory is revisited in the first part of this article, as an explanation of pundits' concerns with the low level of bond yields. The second part explores possible challenges to this prevailing paradigm of assessing bond yields.

~

Information efficiency & breadth of USTs

US Treasuries (USTs) are a particularly information efficient market. This stems from the size of the UST market, and the huge number of institutional participants in the market. The market also has significant breadth, in the sense that various types of investors, including sovereign wealth funds, central banks, pension funds, insurance companies, banks, asset managers and even hedge funds are active market players. As such, the institutional tilt towards bond investing is very high, and direct retail participation is very limited. In the bond market, circa 20% of direct retail participation as in Italy's case, is considered very high, while in other developed economies retail participation is typically under 5% of the respective bond markets. In the US, the large capital gains in USTs over 2012 have raised the participation rate by the retail market to about 10%, and was considerably less (6-8%) in preceding years. Assuming that institutional investors are sophisticated experts, one could deduce that in a market with a larger share of organised investing groups, which are more likely able to assimilate and process information more quickly and effectively, information efficiency in that market would rise in tandem.

In 2012, the size of the global bond market exceeded 100 trillion US dollars, a new record, of which roughly a third was dominated by the US. In comparison, the size of the global equity market was slightly over 50 trillion US dollars. By the scale of the market, we can see why USTs are often seen as a proxy to global risk moves, and signals whether the market is in a "risk-off" or "risk-on" phase. In fact, given the declining effectiveness of the VIX, a volatility index of the S&P 500 to gauge risk appetite, the UST market could very well be a better gauge of global market sentiment. The decline in the effectiveness of VIX has been discussed from various angles, such as the oddity of it declining on a trend basis, reaching new historical lows despite vast fluctuations in risk appetite, a generally sporadic reactivity, and the fact that the VIX is based on the implied volatility of S&P 500 options. On the last point, the problem lies in both the implied nature and limited breadth of the VIX measure. As such, the VIX may not be reflective of the information impounded in market price changes, and one may be better off by using simple range measures of the spot market.

To clarify information efficiency, this refers to what USTs reflect in the collective thinking of market participants. Like any other market, whether USTs reflect economic reality accurately is another matter. What happens in the US Treasury market has wide-ranging implications throughout all asset classes, from the discount factor used in valuing equities, to the negative correlationship with commodities prices. What the US Treasury market could tell us, is trying to tell us, and its relationship to investors in this part of the world is of particular importance today; particularly with the fall in 10 year UST yields from over 2% in March to the current 1.7%.

Common perception of bond market signals

When we consider the persistently downward trendline, it has often been repeated that current bond yields are in a bubble, at least optically. This sentiment can be attributed to UST yields which continue to reflect multi-decade lows; this can be seen from the fall in the 10-year UST yield from 15.8% in 1981 to the current 1.7%. Despite periods of severe volatility, the downward trend-line over the last few decades is evident. That said, the detection of the next multi-decade trend is not easy and logically cannot be extrapolated from the past, particularly with changes in macro-political and demographic trends. The past can only provide guidance, particularly when the future remains very much inscrutable to most of us at this stage. Based on what we now know, forward economic growth trends are not encouraging, creating tailwinds for low yields.

In this article, part of a series, common perceptions regarding low bond yields will be evaluated. Conventional wisdom will be appraised, in the context of the familiar rationale that bond yields are in a bubble. This will be analysed through several lenses, such as yields being at record lows, the inflation link to yields, the lack of a material term risk premium, deteriorating government and corporate finances and the link to economic growth.

Are yields too low?

Regarding record low yields, this has continued to be a phenomenon whether it is with regards to USTs, corporate bonds, or emerging market debt. Some have viewed this as a negative, being financial repression, where investors' and taxpayers' wealth is being transferred to corporate issuers of bonds and governments, where finances are deteriorating. This situation, however, could be viewed from the angle that the lower yields are needed to give a boost to economic growth and facilitate the flow of credit. In this case, the transfer of wealth need not be a zero-sum game, but rather, an impetus for the efficient allocation of resources, paving the way for synergistic value creation.

The problem of low yields needs to be examined from a few perspectives, particularly from the applicability of traditional theory. The next essay will consider the perspective of utilising inflation as a measure of determining relative value. According to theory, higher inflation should lead to higher bond yields. This needs to be considered in the context of empirical evidence, as well as the definition of high inflation. Has the calculation of high inflation shifted? Is the "average" static? Or does it follow a trend of decline? Similarly, current issues in inflationary trends need to be considered, and whether a low inflation environment, partly perpetuated by the drop in commodities' prices, foretells an end of the commodities supercycle. These issues will, in turn, be linked to how much inflationary forces influence interest rate trends, whether growth trends of today and the foretold recovery will lead to a seachange in bond yields, or whether financial repression and massive government debt is an overarching doctrine being imposed by policymakers around the world.

Essay 6

May 2013

What Bond Yields are Saying (Part 2)

The issue of inflation measurement and assessment is discussed as a problem of configuring bond risk premia. Furthermore, central bank monetary policy may not always have an effective degree of transmission, which should raise similar doubts over its transmission to the bond markets.

Also, variations in economic structure, particularly for developing nations, could also lead to problems in interpreting bond yields as a good measure of an efficient system to measuring the cost of financing. As a potential solution, a focus on behaviorally-based models of assessing market movements should be brought into greater focus. Other factors such as financial demand and supply of securities are also issues beyond fundamental economic assessments used to derive "fair" value bond yields.

~

Introduction & recap

In the first instalment of this series, published in the final week of April, we discussed the information efficiency of the bond market, depicted by both breadth and depth, and a wide range of sophisticated institutional investors as participants. Due to the low yields and bond market rally this year, many investors have become concerned that real returns may be insufficient to fund future spending needs, and that bonds are simply overvalued. In the second part of this series, we discuss the re-interpretation of economic variables and what this means for the bond market participants.

Questioning the economic framework in bond prices

Before deciding if inflation affects bond yields, central bankers tend to have a view with regards to the definition and form of inflation, and whether policy moves would budge depending on the type of inflation.

From a traditional economic viewpoint, policy changes tend to occur particularly if the domestic economy reflects a narrowing or expansion of the output gap with regards to the produce of national participants and institutions. The domestic economy's demand is particularly important to the central bank since policy changes will be able to respond better to controlling internal demand factors, rather than supply factors where a policy change may be futile, especially in cases of a supply shock. However, the interplay between the supply side of the economy and the demand side is not very straightforward, particularly when either aspect could have interdependent effects. As a result, there is no hard and fast rule regarding how much interest rates should react to a change in the demand side of the domestic economy. As such, it is often debatable how much does the source and extent of economic growth affect the central bank's decision. That remains a difficult science to pinpoint, and hence, bond markets tend to focus on the tonality of the central bank's statements.

Thus, evolving beyond neoclassical economics, economic stakeholders have become increasingly concerned with how the behaviour of economic participants responds to the implications of a central bank's statements, or the signals as perceived by the market. What this implies is that the central bank need only provide statements of leaning towards either a rate hike or cut to affect the perception of the market. This is important since the impact of such statements on the bond market would then have a domino effect on credit market yields, the interbank rate, and the cost of financing to users of capital. What this culminates in is the importance of the central bank's signalling effects and how they would be able to influence bond prices.

This also raises the confounding question of whether it is the inflation rate and economic growth which affects the central bank's policy, or the central bank's notions which affect the economy and inflation rate. Regardless, the reflexive character of this relationship suggests a need to analyse markets creatively: bond market participants cannot rely solely on economic data to derive estimates of the forward bond yield, but also need to read between the lines of the intentions of the prevailing hegemony.

How much do other relative variables, such as inflation, matter?

Another factor to consider regarding the disconnect between the real economy and bond yields is the role that inflation actually plays; textbook theories aside.

Unfortunately, there is little empirical evidence that inflation is a major factor in the level of bond yields. During the financial crisis, it was the "fear trade" which dictated the level of yields, and up to now, German two-year yields continue to hover near zero. Given the current dynamics, much of the flow of money depends on the lack of supply of perceived safe haven bonds, versus the increase in supply of funds from monies exiting the riskier economies. A problem with considering inflation as a major determinant in bond yields is that the markets remain clustered with frictions. These frictions are not only in the form of supply-demand gaps between safe haven and risky markets, but also whether global liquidity is matched to the types of instruments being offered. In the bond market, the element of duration requirements from different investors is particularly important, adding to the complication of to matching investors and securities. This is in contrast to the equities market, where an ordinary security is usually perceived to be held in perpetuity. These, alongside other market frictions, play a large role in suggesting that it is difficult to value a bond based on the degree of inflation in an economy, amongst other conventional measures such as the disappearing term risk premium. The decline of this term risk premium and the difficulty of making sense of its meaning is related to how we understand risk fungibility and the relationships between interest rates and inflation.

To explain fungibility, consider investors' tendency to compare bond yields to the inflation rate and equity yields. However, this relative valuation hypothesis needs to be used with caution. First, equity dividend yields cannot be compared to the government rate, and comparison with the corporate bond rate suggests that the equity dividend yield needs to be compared with a security of similar credit rating. Secondly, dividend yields have uncertain payouts, and the denominator used in calculating the dividend yield is a highly volatile stock market valuation. Conversely, bond yields cannot be compared to the inflation rate since, in any case, real returns or inflation-adjusted returns have not been the key determinant of whether investors are willing to place their cash in bonds; if inflation-adjusted returns were indeed a primary factor, then bank deposits and bond funds would probably hardly exist, given negative real returns. What relative valuation studies need to do, is to recognise the value people derive from capital preservation, and also recognise the value being placed on inflation stability.

Similarly linked to inflation, interest rates are often thought of as the major determinant in bond yields. However, this is not always the case. In an economy with an interest rate that is particularly stable, such as in Malaysia, policy interest rates play a limited role in determining the level of bond yields. In recent years, due to the high degree of foreign holdings which is currently about a third of the fixed income market (variations to this figure are dependent on definitional issues), the flow of international funds and the direction of the Ringgit had played a larger role in affecting bond prices. However, despite the volatilities in foreign fund flows and their inherent capriciousness, why do bond yields in Malaysia remain relatively low? Coming back to the US Treasuries (USTs) market provides an important answer – bond yields in Asia, are also dependent on where UST yields are priced at (currently very low), being a spread above the "global risk-free rate" as represented by the USTs.

Essay 7

June 2013

Does it All End in Tears?

Measures of economic quality are often useful in understanding the degree of preference for safe haven bonds. However, whether economic quality or sentiment trumps within the overall narrative are determined by the extent of asset price movements in the traded markets. Furthermore, expected returns by investors are very different from central banks which now pursue quantitative easing on the grounds of managing the real economy.

Although some of these measures are important to the capital markets investors, it is important that we are reminded of an essential purpose of the traded securities markets; that is, matching investments with savings. Again, this brings us to the divergent opinions between those which approach the financial market as a casino and those which see it in functional terms. The high-frequency noises creating nuances in interpretation can often create fierce emotions towards the capital markets, but ultimately, markets are there for a purpose beyond quick trades and quick money.

~

The sharp monetary easing and policies geared toward jumpstarting the economy following the 2007/08 financial crisis were back then deemed insufficient, hence leading to quantitative easing, a new monetary policy toolbox which could theoretically bring down the output gap, by crossing the notional zero boundary between policy rates and even easier monetary policy. Today, questions regarding the sustainability of prolonged liquidity creation by central banks have arisen, following the discomfort with unorthodox monetary policy. This fear of the unknown has been linked to the severity of markets volatility.

In fact, I would be as bold to say that we are in the midst of another mini-crisis, sparked not just by mediocre fundamentals, but by the uncertainties of policymakers' communications. Market moves of more than 20% year-to-date are not uncommon. Have a look at the yen, and the plummet in emerging markets equity indices. Flows and sentiment dominate logic. Asset class correlationships do not seem to make sense, and ironically, the only sense of that would be perennial conundrums being repeated all over again – are we actually in the recovery? Will G3 central banks support or derail the recovery? Or are we back on the see-saw?

First of all, growth in the world and the US remains clearly tepid. In Europe, at least one in four persons are unemployed in Portugal and Spain, and much more in peripheral Europe. Moody's is of the opinion that Greece may still default in the medium term. Over in Japan, where aggressive quantitative easing is rife, the government does not have much of a plan for the future of its real economy, and the loss of its safe haven status in the financial markets is something which I opine the markets have yet to digest fully. Meanwhile, in the US, a 5% unemployment rate in pre-crisis language was deemed bad enough for boosting the crime rate. Never have I seen markets rejoice so much when US unemployment rate had just inched up from 7.5% to 7.6% over the last two readings. It is also odd that risk assets are rallying so much at the prospect of less accommodative policy. We appear oblivious to the fact that the world is still de-leveraging, whether it is out of risk aversion, the repayment of hefty government debt, or through the ageing of global demography.

Inflation, on the other hand, has been suppressed. Commodity prices are low, as evidenced by the fall in the Australian dollar and weak industrial production in China. It is difficult for inflation to be sustained in a period of below average capacity utilisation. The dislocations of the financial sector are still under repair, the banking union in Europe and loss absorption bonds by the Basel regulations suggest that financial sector lending activity will probably be sidelined. How can capacity be fulfilled when banks, despite their long-held relationships, are constrained or reluctant to lend? Where is demand emanating when government debts remain either high or on the rise, and higher taxes nigh? Is it not unsettling that corporate bond markets are chasing down yields when the overall persuasions toward debt financing remain divergent? In short, confidence has yet to fully return.

Ultimately, sub-par growth levels, low inflation, and an uncertain global economic outlook are still in place to keep a lid on bond yields. Risk appetite cannot be sustained without synchronised strength in underlying fundamentals, be it across economic indicators or geographies. Sovereigns cannot 'beggar thy neighbour' out of poor growth through ever lower interest rates and currency competition. Central banks, therefore, still need to help. As such, from the perspective of intended results, the management of bond yields through central bank communications are meant to serve constructive economic policy, and consequently, a derailment of that goal is not the intention of any sane central banker. Central bank goals are very clear, even if the communications are garbled, and the market confused.

Finally, the purpose of the bond market remains intact. Governments and corporations alike need to raise money, be it through boom years or through difficult times. Investors hold bonds for a reason, and for very specific personal needs. Insurance companies and banks still need to match assets with liabilities. Central banks still require bonds to manage liquidity and monetary policy. Governments maintain cross-holdings of bonds for political and economic cohesion. Risk can still be reduced through duration hedging and interest rate swaps. Income through fixed income coupons remain embedded in bond structures; in fact, the capital gains game through yield volatility was never quite the mainstay of overall portfolio returns. Fierce trades are just a morsel in the degustation menu of fixed income returns. As such, the game of leap-frog through ever lower yields despite ever lower ratings in a hunt for performance may just end in tears - but just for some.

Essay 8

July 2013

New Roles of Central Banks & Impact on the Bond Markets

Markets often revolt at policies through severe gyrations. Confusing or hard-to-interpret communications by central banks can cause more harm than good, leading to real effects on the cost of financing within the capital markets. Furthermore, there is likely scepticism whereby policies are created after being poorly-conceived, such as the bailout of US banks at the expense of taxpayers' monies following the 2007/08 Financial Crisis.

Central bank communications, policies and perceived credibility can be separately analysed and imputed to determine directional movements in the capital markets.

~

The market has been pretty volatile of late. In such instances, fair value forecasts mean little, while sentiment trumps forecasts derived from any logical model. However, opportunities are particularly plentiful and often salient during such episodes. In this regard, it is pretty important to understand viewpoints which allow us to understand situations where animal spirits are rife, whether this is justified, and how policymakers feature in financial markets.

Currently, 10-year US Treasury yields are trading at their 2 standard deviation peak of the last 12 months, and this is a simple proxy to understand situations of overselling. Other technical indicators are also at play here, which suggest yield levels are at levels of unlikely occurrence, statistically speaking, at least of a normal distribution style of valuations. Nonetheless, the world we currently live in is far from normal, following a continuous bout of unorthodox monetary policy, first from the US, the EU, UK and Japan. However, what's normal in the current nebulous financial markets are: 1) we are at least out of a financial crisis, or at least that is what we and policymakers like to think; 2) global central banks, regulators and other market watchdogs are monitoring the situation more closely; 3) the crisis is not driven by emerging markets with weak institutional quality and that the developed world have been in a better position to utilise sophisticated mechanisms to stem the bleeding; and 4) growth engines are more diversified in various parts of the world.

What is particularly difficult with today's markets are the fact that central banks and policy pundits play an increasingly important role. With the size of the QE programme in the US, Fed tapering talks, anti-crisis Basel III proponents, the Dodd-Frank Act, variations of Volcker Rule implementation across other parts of the world, anti-derivative, anti-securitisation and anti-proprietary trading sentiment, the role of talking heads is becoming ever more powerful.

Recent market swings have been particularly violent with the exhortations of Ben Bernanke and his plans for an exit strategy for QE (Quantitative Easing). There are many schools of thought on how this could have been handled. Alongside the general theory that the market adjustment mechanism is quick and efficient, it can be deduced that in any case, the requirement for Fed tapering through declining QE intensity would be a necessity and a known factor by the market. Furthermore, it would also be difficult for the central bank to predict a precise timeline as to when and how much a withdrawal of QE would be justified. Thus, the market would be adjusting to the continuous flow of economic data that is incoming, with or without the Federal Reserve making bold statements. This concludes a major part of the reason why the bond market is probably in a current spate of overreaction, where The Fed's communications have added fuel to the fire.

Furthermore, markets have a tendency to react to new catalysts. In this case, the need to wind down easy monetary policy is a "new old" catalyst: it is not particularly new that growth has been picking up and that the global economy is at least limping its way to the economic recovery. This characterisation is more likely than a full-fledged recovery, given sanguine inflation expectations and generally well-contained commodity prices, regardless of idiosyncratic event-driven bumps in oil prices now and then. Based on this, we can then extrapolate that the recent wild swings in the market are not driven by fundamentals or a logical progression of the policy pathway, but rather a confusion over monetary policy direction and policy statements.

On this point, evidence suggests that recent communications in the G3 central banks may have done more harm than good to financial market stability: 1) excessive volatility in bond markets and FX markets following the US central bank's "taper talk" communications; 2) excessive currency depreciation (e.g. greater than 15%) akin to a currency crash in Japan's case.

Based on traditional economics, a key role of a central bank is in conducting monetary policy, and this is a given fact which has been performed with frequent activity in recent years. However, in today's world, monetary policy tools have become far wider, and this includes the relationship that some G3 central banks have with the banking system, particularly in the buy-back of bonds which is related to maintaining the stability of systemically important financial institutions. With this in mind, it is plausible that with this relationship, monetary policy runs the risk of being less independent and political.

However, in carrying out the role of safeguarding financial system stability, central banks also need to remain independent. In the 2007/08 crisis, the nationalisation of banks and the resale of such banks for a profit, also calls into question the independence of central banks, and whether it should be involved in such agency roles. It is also difficult to account if the net benefit of the difference in a bank's pre- and post-crisis valuation is being eventually returned to society with an equivalent utility value.

What this suggests is the potential degradation of the quality of central bank independence, and some misguidance over the clarity of central bank roles, even at some of the advanced economies. While policy transparency and communication is positive, it needs to be done in the context of fulfilling its core roles, such as promoting financial stability. Excessive communications in itself is not a core role. How much central banks are becoming politicised in today's world of increasingly larger financial sectors, and veering off traditional roles, could be inducing both potentially deliberate and inadvertent volatility of the unwelcome kind in financial markets.

Essay 9

August 2013

Constructive Ambiguity

Information transparency can function in perverse ways. On one hand, it helps promote trust which underpins all transactions on which a social contract is built, particularly for financial markets. However, assuming a utilitarian view, too much information, especially that which leaves room for misinterpretation, could lead to a miscoordination in the financial markets, spiralling into adverse herd behaviour.

However, what's more important is the initiation and entrenchment of accurate and transparent information. A market in which expectations are homogeneously and unrealistically sanguine, creates a problem whereby the result of a risk event becomes binary. In other words, risk can turn extremely negative and systemic in the event false perceptions are widely shared and similar. A good example where this concept is manifested is with the AAA CDO (Collateralised Debt Obligation) market, a key cause of the 2007/08 Financial Crisis.

~

Fitch's recent outlook downgrade on Malaysia has been premised largely on public finance concerns, such as the high level of government debt and a narrow tax base. These are usually regarded in themselves as sovereign risk factors, akin to the financial ratios which are evaluative of private firms' creditworthiness. In more formal jargon, these are specific or idiosyncratic risks, as opposed to systematic or non-diversifiable risks.

Concerning this, global bond yields have been rising and as such, risk factors are being re-examined, overshadowing the focus on potential returns; as markets capitulate, the focus is on the downside. Across several asset classes, we have been worried about "fully valued" markets. Thus, what, in today's terms, have caused downside risks to rise and upside potential to decline? The current focus on the rise in yields is often attributable to systematic risks arising from external factors such as a deterioration in current account deficits, and in Malaysia's case, a less optimistic outlook on its public finances. The "great rotation" has also been discussed, consistent with the idea that Asian economies are not as rich in current account surpluses and foreign exchange reserves as they once were. Capital imports, aggressive spending on infrastructure, and a fall in export values have contributed to this. Furthermore, a recovery in the developed markets and the potential tapering off in expansionary monetary policy is beginning to spook markets, attracting emerging markets liquidity to economies such as the Eurozone, Japan and the US.

Hence, an examination of such risks through these lens seem to consider risks within a traditional multi-factor asset pricing framework, akin to a checklist approach to risks pertaining to those specific to only securities and those about the wider macroeconomy.

However, the flow of risks through time is infinitely more complex and shifts unpredictably upon different variables and at different stages. One such time-varying risk would be the situation of information asymmetry within the debt markets, and how this is related to tail risks.

It has been widely discussed that a major cause of the 2007/08 credit crisis in the US was due to the shadow banking system in the form of a large asset-backed securities market. Consider the collateralised debt obligation (CDO), which essentially transforms the credit ratings of less creditworthy obligors, into high grade ratings with strong demand, via the CDO repackaging and tranching process. The CDO repackaging process also facilitates liquidity, transforming illiquid loans to tradeable debt, or bonds. A second reason why this is done is to enhance access to funding for companies with weaker credit scores. However, this causes problems since the credit transformation process results in an obscuring of credit information where a large number of debtors are processed through a conduit to produce securities of better ratings than what they originally were. Here, the information frictions arise because the capability to monitor hundreds of transactions underlying a single CDO package can be called into question. Furthermore, the CDO transaction is also subject to model risk, particularly with the uncertainties that fat-tailed distributions bring. There exist other information frictions such as operational monitoring issues ex-post of the CDO issuance, but we shall not discuss this in detail here.

Consequently, apart from the usual consideration of evaluating credit risk, the problem here at its core, is related to monitoring, information asymmetry, and information opacity problems.

Dang, Gorton and Holmström (2009)[1] explained deliberate information opacity as an inherent result of developed debt markets:

"Trade is best implemented by debt which preserves ignorance because it provides the smallest incentive for private information production, which creates adverse selection. Debt's value is also least sensitive to public signals. In this economy policies that increase transparency would reduce welfare. Finally, even if there is adverse selection in the market, debt maximises the amount of trade. For the economy as a whole there is a systemic risk of using debt to provide liquidity: an aggregate shock, if bad enough, can be made worse by triggering private information production, causing adverse selection when debt becomes information-sensitive."

---

[1]Dang, T. V., Gorton, G., & Holmstrom, B. (2009).'Opacity and the optimality of debt for liquidity provision'. *Manuscript Yale University.*

In our earlier example, we discussed the CDO, a private sector cause of the 2007/08 systemic crisis. With this and the above excerpt in mind, let us explore the parallels between this problem and the rest of the bond market, including public sector bonds.

In a highly geared economy, the theory suggests that negative public signals should best be avoided. This can be understood from the perspective of bank runs since bond investors can be likened to "depositors" while an en masse withdrawal is akin to a "bank run". The only difference is that the bond market is, in a greater proportion, part of the shadow banking system rather than the traditional banking system. However, as Dang, Gorton and Holmström (2009) suggested, this can only be helpful up to the point where bond markets are of sanguine sentiment, before a search for information causes market dislocations.

The question here is: what causes debt markets to be less sensitive to public information? This can occur when credit risk information is perceived as homogeneous, for example, when the credit market is viewed as an undifferentiated blanket of investable ratings, for reasons such as sanguine sentiment. Furthermore, the condition of preserving ignorance occurs when homogeneity in creditworthiness perceptions leads to homogeneity in expectations and known information, since homogeneous ignorance is a form of information symmetry. As such, it follows that information symmetry, facilitates trading liquidity, at least to the point at which market conditions are stable. When market conditions are unfavourable, such as when bond yields are rising, it will lead to the demand for private information production, which causes a breakdown in the publicly intended signal of sanguinity. Subsequently, this is where unrealised risks morph into an exacerbated systemic risk. This phenomenon can occur in bond markets where rising yields lead to the need for investors to justify credit reasons to hold a bond, and when the scrutiny on investments rise during periods of increased paranoia. In summary, when risk perceptions are similar, systemic risks are exaggerated when they materialise.

Similarly, when a homogeneously large proportion of high grade bonds and a larger portion of government debt, including implicitly supported or government-guaranteed debt, begins to eclipse other components of the private sector bond market, the maintenance of ignorant information symmetry not only arises out of an inability to differentiate risk, but also the obvious limits to information forthcoming from the bureaucratic machinery of government. Again, due to homogeneity of perceived credit risk, this can cause the large adverse jump from unrealised risks to systemic non-diversifiable risk. The even more difficult exercise in this, is factoring in the risk premium to be priced in bonds of this nature, since its cause is situational on whether additional information is demanded.

Essay 10

September 2013

How Risky is a QE Taper for Asian Markets Today?

Quantitative easing (QE) is a variant of easy monetary policy; hence, there are concerns over its continued use given the risk of creating excessive inflation and an asset bubble. QE is viewed with suspicion since it does not operate traditionally via interest rates, but through the bond market which results in decisions which are both aided and convoluted by the collective wisdom of markets.

However, QE was also used at a time when interest rates were already low and orthodox interest rate policy was viewed to be ineffective during the crisis of 2007/08; the policy arose partly due to lack of a choice. Back then, the crisis had its origins in the credit markets and hence, a rationale could have been the use of a policy tool which addressed capital markets problems directly. The pros and cons of QE should continue to be explored, and with any macroeconomic policy, should not be expected to operate with full optimality across all time periods. Kudos should be given for policy innovation and situational policymaking, since economic crises are never identical across time, suggesting a constant need to remodel outdated theories.

~

I had previously discussed concerns over the sustainability of easy monetary policy and whether this may need to be eventually reversed. One of the concerns was whether the sharp easing of monetary policy following the 2007/08 financial crisis would be mirrored by an equally sharp tightening of monetary policy when the time is right. However, whether the time is right continues to be a point of confusion for the bond markets, and moves in excess of 10bps a day are not uncommon.

Perhaps the unusual urge to do something about the state of monetary policy today has much to do with the suspicion towards unorthodox monetary policy. It is likely that both central bankers and academics find it cognitively jarring to practice a science that has yet to be empirically proven as sound. Prolonged quantitative easing was enacted when markets were faced with the meltdown, and due to the perception that recovery has occurred, the earnest need to unwind such policy is starting to be felt.

Given this notion, it is highly likely that markets continue to face increased risk premiums due to various forms of uncertainty. Firstly, quantitative easing has proven to be effective following a severe crisis, but the ex-post effects remain very much untested. Traditional economic theory suggests that this may eventually lead to high inflation. However, severe global inflation has not been a major policy problem for quite some time, with the global CPI in the low teens during the turn of the decade beginning in 1980.

There are some strands of thought which could be related to the ability of central banks to maintain easy policy. Firstly, technological advancements have allowed a more effective matching of demand with supply, helping smooth out structural frictions which can lead to cost-pushed inflation. For example, inventory planning has become more effective, which in turn has positive effects in lessening supply shocks. Secondly, policymakers have become a lot more wary of asset price bubbles, since this happened during accelerating commodities prices and high real estate prices during the prelude to the 2007/08 Great Recession. Commodity prices currently, are showing signs of stability particularly with the public communications policy of the Chinese government in promoting sustainable and quality growth, rather than a rapid pace of expansion.

Nonetheless, my experience with investors is that empirical evidence and numbers tend to have a greater impact on financial activity and prices. It is not easy to sell the nebulous idea that a rise in total factor productivity and potential GDP growth capacity would then lead to a shrinkage of bottlenecks which are particularly prone to causing inflation.

Hence, the spectre remains that sharply higher inflation could happen if money supply and credit growth rises should easy monetary policy be continuously pursued. Then, it would be difficult to put forth the argument that: i) more risk averse and pessimistic consumers; ii) bank hoarding behaviour; and iii) a lack of the equitable and required distribution of credit, will continue to crimp overall levels of demand and continue to maintain an output gap.

Given this backdrop, the fear that US Treasury yields and US interest rates will rise presents another uncertainty for investors. This uncertainty has continued to be compounded given questions over US Federal Reserve regarding the degree and timing of a tapering of Quantitative Easing. The candidacy for the next Federal Reserve Chairman, arguably the most powerful person in the financial world, also remains fraught with rumour and uncertainty. The withdrawal of Lawrence Summers from the candidacy with Janet Yellen again at the forefront is a very telling sign of the preference for markets and stakeholders to ensure that monetary policy continues to remain easy. The rally of relief by bond markets is a testament to this, so was the recent Fed meeting which suggested an overall dovish tone. Furthermore, another fact to consider is whether the applause by the bond markets are indicative of the final candidate for the position or otherwise is unclear, and given cause-effect circularity in the financial markets, I would not dare to commit whether it is the financial markets which lead position fulfillment at the US Federal Reserve or vice versa.

However, what is important is that US Fed Policy is conducted responsibly. While some quarters are concerned over the dovish-hawkish flip-flopping in tone at the US central bank, I suggest that these need to be brushed aside with an open mind. Ultimately, we do not want to see a derailment of the US recovery. There is no benefit should a spike in US rates lead to a sharp emerging markets meltdown. With continued surplus and creditor status of the developing world, the symbiotic relationship between emerging market lenders and the G3 economies as borrowers remain strong.

Thus, the notion that Asia could eventually slip into another 1997/98-style Asian Financial Crisis is likely untrue on account of the want and need of central banks to seal a global economic recovery. Furthermore, a key element of the 1997/98 Asian Financial Crisis was the presence of misguided currency policy, where pegged exchange rates and a subsequently futile defence through the depletion of precious foreign exchange reserves allowed speculative attacks on currencies to occur. Up to this day, the difficulty of enacting this is being safeguarded by policy defences, such as partial pegs to "secret" baskets of currencies, the flexibility to impose partial restrictions on flows of "hot" money and a currency-defence fund in the form of the Chiang Mai Initiative, amongst others. On a fundamental level, most Asian economies would likely end the year with surpluses. A decline in current account surpluses should not be seen with undue pessimism and should not be equated to a deficit. A decline in surpluses can impact financial securities' prices but is fundamentally insufficient to warrant a systemic crisis. Loans to deposit ratios are still below 100% today, vis-à-vis above 100% for several countries such as Hong Kong, Indonesia, South Korea, Singapore, and Malaysia before the Asian Financial Crisis. Other measures in ASEAN, such as foreign exchange reserves to imports, remain in a healthy position at more than five times, while government debt comprises less than half of GDP on average.

Essay 11

October 2013

A Constructive Warning from US Political Brinksmanship

Economic and financial hegemony changes, and should not be relied upon as a permanent strength of any particular economy. In fact, such assumptions could lead to moral hazard which can lead to complacency, entitlement, and an eventual erosion of the initially enjoyed influence. This power can be modelled as a stock of benefits derived from financial access and flexibility of reserve currency economies, and the benefitting nations in this respect need to preserve the use of this resource lest the emergence of a tragedy of the commons.

~

Capital markets heaved a sigh of relief when the US government managed to postpone its debt ceiling decision on 16th October, even though this will need to be revisited on the 7th of February. Reaching a grand bargain now appears to be even more of wishful thinking as political bickering remains a constant problem under President Obama's administration.

An overarching question regarding the can kicking has to do with the potential reaction from rating agencies. In 2011, Standard and Poor's downgraded the US' AAA rating by a notch to AA+, given similar conditions of political dysfunction in Congress. This was with regard to the political brinksmanship in the US which was seen to be an erosion of institutional strength and credibility. As we can see, for an economy such as the US which relies heavily on its privilege as a global economic and political hegemon with reserve currency status for cheap funds, it is quite likely that normative qualitative factors such as policy-making effectiveness and efficiency are likely to play an important role in assessing the sovereign rating. In addition, it is also uncertain if the US would be able to sustain debt levels via new revenue options and work towards consolidating public sector finances given rising healthcare and social security expenses in a period when winning votes remain an important goal of politicians. However, not all rating agencies view this situation similarly; for example, Fitch had in 2011, refrained from taking a rating action during the same debt ceiling debate back then, citing the economy's wealth, diversification and dynamism. However, Fitch has finally placed the US economy on negative outlook on 15-October-2013, which is likely due to the repeat of US political dysfunction. Meanwhile, Moody's rating actions have been more optimistic, having raised the US outlook from negative to stable, citing a decline in the fiscal deficit-to-GDP ratio from 7% in 2012 to 4% in 2013 which is a surprisingly better improvement.

As such, it is apparent that the three major rating agencies have different views with regards to the sovereign credit quality of the US economy, and this is dependent on how much weight has been given to institutional and political credibility as opposed to meeting public sector financial ratio targets. Nonetheless, it is important to take a step back, and view the rating from a long term view. While the rating agencies' actions suggests divisions over the "correct" rating of the US economy, long-term trends such as the diversification of reserves away from the US dollar and capital market participants mulling the eventual rise of China as a global reserve currency, suggest that the reserve currency status of the US as a lynchpin to its high credit rating is increasingly under threat. Furthermore, there is a symbiotic relationship between the extent of global hegemonic and political credibility with the confidence that capital markets place on any reserve currency. Given the lack of an alternative, and the institutionalised entrenchments for the use of the US dollar within global trade and financing, it is unlikely that the reserve currency status of the US would change anytime soon, even though this has become a pertinent consideration as compared to such an idea being unheard of a decade ago.

Against this backdrop, it is also important to consider the potential merits of the world becoming more aware that an overreliance on the US dollar should be avoided. Firstly, the gradual and insidious erosion of the quality of the US sovereign rating and the long-term value of the US dollar, could presage heightened reinvestments into the real economy. Consequently, this could spur growth in the exports sector and reduce a disproportionately large financial sector which the US has used too much of as a crutch to grow its GDP and maintain its status as global hegemon. Furthermore, this could result in a reduction of global systemic risks which are embedded in too-big-to-fail systemically important financial institutions and the financial system of the US. Finally, moral hazard could be reduced when there is a decline in the captive demand and excessive supply of money by the US via the US debt and currency markets. With this decline in moral hazard, the privilege to print debt with impunity would erode, hence inevitably assisting in the debt reduction and rebalancing process of global deficits and surpluses.

Therefore, it is important that global policymakers enter new eras with fresh mindsets. In the past, the control for military strength has always been at the top of sovereigns' agendas, to conquer as much geographical area as possible to gain access to vital human capital and natural resources. In modern times, financial warfare can be seen in the culmination of the US as global reserve currency, a result of power relations via the financial markets. Nonetheless, as we can now see, a lopsided concentration of economic power carries with it a host of idiosyncratic risks and uncertainties for the world. If the stockpile of sovereign risk and commensurate return is limited globally, having one party dominate this is equivalent to exploiting a shared capital market resource akin to a tragedy of the commons problem. Similarly, having a reserve currency being vested within a single economy can be likened to a situation of self-interest whereby a non-cooperative disequilibrium occurs. Ultimately, as emerging economies mature, financial architecture in the future should consider the benefits of facilitating a coordinated and near-optimal Nash equilibrium in currency and bond markets whereby no single party ends up with a too-big-to-fail reserve currency. Assuming society's predilection for net global benefits supported by cooperative ideals, aided by the recently dented confidence for laissez-faire capitalism, perhaps some optimism over a less monopolistic global currency and bond market can be warranted for the distant future.

Essay 12

February 2014

What Makes a Crisis?

Can both markets and economic turbulence be seen as a deterministic process, especially when they cannot be specifically attributed to economic factors but rather the effects of flawed policies? To begin with, the factors expressing negative events are of varying weights and ultimately depend on a narrative being provided to that cluster of factors which are deemed to cause vulnerabilities. Additionally, there is the issue of the dichotomy between localised and generalised markets malaise. It could be crudely simplified that national political events tend to have a limited cross-border effect unlike economic cycles and capital movements which are bound by time rather than space.

~

The recent sell down in the emerging markets has raised the spectre of a potential emerging capital markets crisis, denting confidence after at least half a decade of Goldilocks economies in the developing world. In the bond markets in particular, the sanguine conditions were of course, bolstered by mild commodities prices, a lack of demand pressures on inflation, and highly friendly fiscal and monetary policies from regulators and governments.

While traditional ideas of capital market cycles tie in with the macroeconomic theory of business cycles, in that booms and busts are inescapable, it is perhaps more useful for practitioners to dissect the actual elements of a crisis to understand the forms and evolution of crises, which can be helpful to market timing decisions.

These ideas can be viewed through the lens of macroeconomics, politics and financial markets.

With regards macroeconomics, the recent sell down in markets has affected the Fragile Five most saliently – Brazil, Indonesia, India, South Africa and Turkey. There are two schools of thought regarding the Fragile Five's vulnerabilities. The fundamental rationale is that these economies face current account deficits and high inflation, which brings back memories of the 1997/98 emerging markets crisis. However, the crux of the 1997/98 crisis was substantially rooted in mismanaged economic policy, where exchange rates were pegged. In the theory of the trilemma, an economy cannot, without consequences, pursue a combination of independent monetary policy, fixed exchange rates and an open capital account. Back in 1997/98, economic policies at several EM countries were inappropriately positioned, where fixed or largely pegged currencies resulted in central banks having to deplete foreign exchange reserves to defend a targeted exchange rate. As a result, the balance of payments deficit got worse, since the lack of currency depreciation meant that the trade account could not rebalance positively to plug the deficit. Today, in 2014, these economies do not face the problem of an inflexible currency regime.

However, another element which contributed to the 1997/98 financial crisis was the lack of adequate governance and risk management standards in the banking system. Problems of the banking system, on the other hand, are much more difficult to resolve, being in the private sector, protected by its charter of developing financial markets, assisting GDP growth, special role of matching savers with investors in the economy, and too-big-to-fail status. Today, I opine that global standards of governance and risk management have improved, but ultimately, when there's a will, there's a way, for moral hazard, rent seeking and greed to come into the picture; that, I am unable to offer constructive insight.

Then, from an economic cycle perspective, the generally accepted proposition for a more negative outlook is related to the fact that the Goldilocks conditions of balanced growth and inflation is fading, signalled by the US central bank gradually phasing out its quantitative easing programme. As such, higher implied rates and a shrinking of the carry trade would then reverse the massive accumulation of capital inflows by the emerging markets.

However, consider some opposing arguments to this: i) G3 unemployment is still very high, and despite incremental growth rates being largely contributed by the developing economies, the G3 still comprises about a quarter of total world GDP, which then implies that global monetary conditions would still be considerably accommodative; ii) commodities prices are mild which may constrain cost-push pressures, particularly after the build-up in capacity during the commodity boom years of the mid-2000s; and iii) even if G3 interest rates were to rise by 1%, absolute interest rates and investment yields at the emerging economies would still be higher on average, which is supportive of continued carry trade activity.

Macroeconomic arguments aside, the recent market jitters are probably just as political as it is economic in nature. In South Africa, the African National Congress remains very much entrenched with the existence of polarising politics, with the old guard such as existing industry unions unable to make way for a true realisation of liberty and democratic market reforms. At the same time, the ideology of rebels is unable to support economic progress with nationalisation and expropriation policies being mooted. In Turkey, the Prime Minister has been seen as unreasonable through the use of gag politics tactics and hostility toward foreign investments. In Brazil, Dilma Rousseff has been seen as more interventionist as opposed to market-driven, although alternative parties can be even more socialist in nature. In India, weaknesses in the real economy and current account have been rooted in issues of corruption and governance, where the central bank, despite being under illustrious leadership, has limited influence. Like India, Indonesia also faces general elections in 2014 by the middle of the year. At best, we can hope for a lack of hampering politics which could derail plans at narrowing twin deficits, although healthier long-term prospects for the Indonesian and Indian economies may very well ease potential difficulties in political transition.

Given the nature of localised political issues and the disparate bodies of risk-off behaviour in the recent bout of market panic, we at least do not see strong evidence of a common macro risk factor which could morph recent market concerns into one of wider systemic risk. Furthermore, at least empirically, what we see is a lack of a correlated risk-off sentiment across geographical markets, asset classes and sectors. That said, if a crisis does occur, it usually occurs as a curve ball thrown in the face of investors by the markets, but based on what we now know, the portents of another 1997/98 or 2007/08 style crisis recurring appears quite unlikely, at least for the year ahead.

Essay 13

April 2014

A New Global Central Bank Regime?

The role of a central banker is not an easy one. On one hand, institutions and committee structures are meant to regulate decisions and to prevent awry policy. On the other hand, it is not uncommon for varying levels of scepticism as to whether these institutional structures can create objective processes leading to objective measures. For one, the representation of a scientific paradigm does not necessarily impose or cultivate any form of objectivity. Central bank decisions are both an art and science, and even one's psychological context will be brought to bear in the markets' interpretation of policy matters. Human passions, historical context and even fate are often weighed in what is very much a social construct.

~

Recent posturing by newly inaugurated US Federal Reserve Chairman Janet Yellen sheds considerable light on the coming shape of global monetary policy. On this issue, it is worth placing a judgment on market reactions regarding her stand on monetary policy, how this has shifted, as well as the key indicators which hold dear to Yellen's formation of views regarding the economy. In addition, with the US being a major centre of gravity defining the contours of global monetary policy, it is a worthwhile exercise for Asia-Pacific financial markets to shape investing expectations in line with issues of external vulnerability and global capital flows.

The initial stand on Yellen by the financial markets was the likelihood of her having a more dovish personality. However, this has gradually changed over time with some market commentators believing in the need for her to prove a steely edge to her policy construction views. Nonetheless, this is hardly sound guidance for judging Yellen's longer-term stance on policy matters, given her responsibility to guide the US as a major driver of the world economy and financial markets. Such financial market beliefs are probably useful for short-term trading ideas, but in the medium to long term, major shifts in market valuations or the framework of valuations ranges depend on whether a catalytic regime change has occurred.

Exploring this notion, we need to remember that Yellen remains bound by her responsibilities as a central banker, and what may have made her appear dovish, is at least partly framed by the context of the current economic regime and state of global economic recovery. For the US government and for the purpose of fulfilling her role appropriately, a dovish tilt may be required, driven more by macroeconomics rather than her individual personality or her solid academic background in labour market economics. Regardless, her deep understanding of labour market conditions and the problems behind the statistics will be useful wisdom in guiding her policy thoughts. To be pragmatic, markets must then adapt their reactions to this wisdom rather than criticise it. On this note, this is where a "regime change" is likely a better description of the markets-to-central bank interaction, rather than a simplistic characterisation of Yellen being a "dove" or "hawk".

Yellen, in her speech as of 31st March, was particularly concerned not just with the level of unemployment, but also the nature of unemployment. In this respect, she was reinforcing her earlier view that an explicit unemployment rate target for the purpose of policy setting may be impractical. Based on my interpretation, Yellen was concerned that the unemployment rate was not very informative of structural unemployment caused by supply-demand mismatching of human resources. She mentioned there were difficulties in labour market participants who have lost their job following the Great Recession, and that employers were averse to hiring those who have been out of a job for more than six months. As such, the effect of a recession may then add to structural unemployment numbers simply because of the time it takes for businesses to recover during which long-term unemployed numbers continue to rise. Technological changes, industry changes and the existence of marginalised communities also remain part of the unemployment problem. It is with such examples, that Yellen highlights the need to see past the headline employment statistics, to understand that high structural employment may be persistent. Thus, it is probably wise for Yellen to avoid guiding the market of potential policy changes based on the mechanical tracking of a headline statistic that does not represent a multi-faceted truth.

Furthermore, labour market conditions cannot be determined solely by the unemployment rate, but also the level of wage growth which Yellen highlighted. According to Yellen, wages have risen by a mere 2% per annum since the recession. In addition, the labour market participation rate has fallen from 66% to 63%. In totality, this appears to imply a level downshift in confidence both for those seeking employment and employers.

To gauge future policy moves, it is also important to note Yellen's belief that central bank policy is more useful in bringing down the cyclical component of unemployment to the long-term sustainable level. In formal terms, this is the NAIRU – non-accelerating inflation rate of unemployment, which is the rate at which the unemployment rate can be sustained without accelerating inflation above neutral. The current expectation of this level by the Federal Reserve is 5.2% to 5.6%, which is still quite a distance away from the 6.7% headline unemployment rate recorded in February. As such, 1.1% to 1.5% of slack in the labour markets still needs to be resolved. Based on the current unemployment rate, the projected level for a sustainable level, and other labour statistics such as wage growth, the participation rate, and long-term unemployed, another 12 months could easily pass before we see a shift to less accommodative policy.

On the international markets, what this suggests is that the carry trade will likely remain alive for a while, and that capital inflows into higher yielding emerging markets is unlikely to suddenly halt. Without a major shift in tone of US monetary policy, it is also unlikely for other weakened G10 economies to participate in a self-defeating shift to monetary policy contraction. On US Treasuries, the backing down of 10-year yields has already priced in some of the practical difficulties in raising interest rates and tightening monetary policy unnecessarily.

Ultimately, whether a central bank follows a rules-based or discretionary interest rate policy remains both a perennial and moot argument, as the format is usually dependent on prevailing economic conditions with a mix of the two formats. Factors which may be considered include the need to maintain credibility, beliefs of incumbent monetary policy committee members, historical precedence and the severity of expansionary or contractionary conditions that the central bank is trying to address. Perhaps a degree of constructive ambiguity is appropriate to the current management of unprecedented and unorthodox monetary policy.

Essay 14

May 2014

Thoughts on Risks

Financial markets can be geographically analysed, as each region contributes to a set of specific risks which are in turn placed as an undercurrent contributing to the overall level of risk. While it can be proposed that risks originate by place, the generalising element of information opacity and asymmetry creates integrating rather than differentiating forces in the materialisation of risks. It is often thought that monetary policy and excessive liquidity combined with the conduit of the financial markets has encouraged cohesion of risks emanating from separate geographies, although where the lines of risks are blurred depend on the interpreter of information, that is, by investors at varying levels of understanding. In this case, the use of information is segmented with varied levels of derived utility.

~

The initial expectation of the market was one of sustained growth in the US, although this has been partly diluted by both internal and external concerns. The internal concerns were well-articulated by Janet Yellen, who mentioned her main concern with structural unemployment. On this matter, the solution is unlikely to remain solely in the hands of the Federal Reserve, as long-term internal balance requires far greater efforts in the supply-side of the economy, such as the optimality of the composition of national output and productivity. Although the supply-side solution mostly lies in the hands of politicians and fiscal policy, what monetary policy can do for now is to ensure that credit conditions are conducive to maintaining the healthy trajectory of consumer sentiment we have been seeing in the US.

While the ideal circumstance is for policymakers to encourage private sector lending throughout the economy, whether this occurs is a function of risk management practices as well as competitive pressures. As it stands, banks remain under the scrutiny of regulators despite the improvement of credit scores for consumers given the gradually recovering employment market in the US. As such, the US economy is far from being wildly optimistic, and this scenario is probably more conducive for sustained growth rates going forward, as policy makers tread cautiously and remain accommodative.

In the meantime, the European economies continue to stage a gradual and slow recovery, boosted by friendly monetary policy which is in turn helped by very low levels of inflation of under 1%. Nonetheless, all is not well in peripheral Europe, with recent news of instabilities in the Greek government, and the need to plug capital holes in Greek banks' balance sheets. As it stands, much of the growth acceleration continues to emanate from Germany, and greater awareness needs to be shared with regards to the distribution of wealth within European countries and across the European Union. That said, the recent reaction of bond yields appear to be generally benign, with very limited spillover of Greece's sovereign risk to the rest of peripheral Europe.

Concurrently, investors need to remain vigilant of global events, particularly with the overhanging fear of tail risks from the emerging markets: i) the Ukrainian geopolitical crisis; ii) credit quality strains at the sovereign level for Brazil, Argentina and Venezuela; recall that these Latin American economies are known to be serial defaulters throughout history, with a poor record of policy credibility; and iii) defaults in China wealth management products and uncertainties over the sustainability of shadow banking.

Collectively, we can see that these tail risks are not related to traditional measures of economic fundamentals, such as a balance of payments imbalance and debt levels. With this in mind, it is also incorrect to believe that with stable to improving macroeconomic fundamentals, a crisis cannot occur. In fact, crises have a tendency to occur when it is least expected, and when a trigger event which may or may not be related to economic fundamentals causes market panic, a self-fulfilling unwinding of long positions occur.

Additionally, it is usually not the "knowns" that should be feared, but the "unknowns" that markets are unprepared for. In this regard, a worrying trend to be noted in the markets is the lack of credit due diligence we have seen, particularly at private banks of regional financial centres. Again, the problem here arises from information asymmetry between the more informed credit sellers as compared to buyers. However, this form of asymmetry is unlike usual forms where the information cost leads to profit opportunities for credit sellers; in this case, the asymmetry is compounded when buyers lack resources to conduct sufficient credit research, and select credits based solely on the return objective. Thus, risk sensitivity is greatly diminished and this can cause a misallocation of capital to companies which may not deserve it. The information problem has also heightened as a result of instrument complexity. Through my recent observations, I note that purchasers, especially the retail segment, are not pricing Basel III bank securities accurately, without sufficient yields or returns compensating for adopting higher structural risks. Furthermore, the issuance of junk bonds, covenant-light and exotic structures has been rising, alongside a perplexing decline in credit spreads (i.e. a decline in *required* rates of return).

The worrying nature of this development is even greater, considering the rise in debt refinancing needs. Anecdotal evidence suggests that declining lending capacity at banks has caused a rise in disintermediation, that is, the growth of the bond market. While disintermediation is often discussed in positive terms of capital markets development and liberalisation, the sinister side of this is tightening risk management guidelines driven by both bank credit officers and financial system supervisors. In other words, are public credit markets becoming too lax with assessing credit risks as compared to private debt lending? Do banks fear what credit markets have turned a blind eye to?

Thus, it can be seen that the liquidity creation and accommodative policies of central banks have led to the disregard of information asymmetries in the pricing of risks. For investors, remedies to be suggested include: i) ensuring that credit risks are priced on a fundamental level, rather than being largely priced off the volatile government yield curve; ii) the government yield curve especially in safe havens will likely rise from its current low base; even though this may be slow and gradual, credit portfolios which are inherently less liquid need to price in exit flexibilities; iii) active management, credit and alpha strategies need to take precedence, particularly when yield curve risk is largely a given; iv) scrutiny over credit and macroeconomic fundamentals which are largely healthy may yield inconclusive results as opposed to being on high alert for behavioural disequilibria.

Essay 15

June 2014

Taxation Policy & Sovereign Credit Quality

In my opinion, tax policies and the robustness of tax revenues are quite an important element of sovereign credit analysis. However, this aspect is often neglected when compared to static measures such as government debt-to-GDP and the fiscal deficit. Tax revenues are to a government, what operating cash flows are to a corporate. Without the analysis of this flow measure, sovereign credit analysis could become lopsidedly pessimistic in which future government earnings are not given due credit; conversely, inaccuracies in government cash flow forecasting is also a risk.

~

Amongst other elements, tax policy is probably the most directly linked to assessing an economy's pathway toward debt sustainability. Taxation essentially determines the extent to which the government can raise revenues to repay its expenses. In business terms, it is akin to the "sales" or "revenues" of a government, and an excess of tax revenues over public sector costs are important to maintain tenable sovereign credit quality.

In our work for assessing sovereign credit quality, the government's revenue-to-cost ratio can be utilised to assess expectations of future government surpluses or deficits, of which taxation revenues play an integral role. At a quantitative macroeconomic level, sovereign credit analysts are particularly concerned with the extent to which a country's GDP per capita is sufficient to provide a tax base, which is in turn related to the depth of the economy. Unlike most other forms of economic analysis which is more concerned with rate of change data such as GDP growth, GDP per capita for taxation and sovereign credit analysis, is more important since it not only inform us of wealth levels, but also indicates the level quality of life and the effectiveness of the government's macroeconomic management.

In this regard, and from a qualitative viewpoint, a low level of GDP per capita could be indicative of deep-seated problems such as low education levels, weak institutions, inconsistent policies and poor infrastructure in an economy which is negative for potential GDP expansion. Such economies are also often plagued with a large informal sector, whereby the penetration rate of tax collection is relatively low.

However, it may be easier to reconcile the fact that developing economies which are often resource-based tend to have problems with regards to bringing tax-to-GDP levels up to an acceptable level, than trying to appraise the endogenous reasons for dismal credit quality and tax collection levels. To explain, resource-rich economies which are developing, tend to be more export-oriented with a low composition of the services sector within overall GDP. At the same time, customs taxes and other tariff or non-tariff barriers tend to create distortions due to several reasons, such as the difficulty of ascertaining the optimal trade barrier, the economic rationale and price of the taxation, as well as the presence of corruption and rent-seeking behaviour at collection or processing points.

Furthermore, it may be difficult for developing economies to broaden the tax base due to the relatively smaller size of GDP which makes them beholden to the vicissitudes of global trade for economic sustenance. Additionally, in line with the stereotype of "resource-cursed" countries, diversification of economic sectors to broaden the tax base can be difficult due to inherent behavioural factors such as moral hazard of depending on prior and existing resource-based wealth. Given this backdrop, another dilemma is presented – if it is optimal that all economies endogenously diversify, does that not refute the theory of trade specialisation and its accompanying gains via positive externalities?

Apart from a somewhat dismal outlook for some economies which appear to lack a way out from experiencing poor government finances due to institutional weaknesses, corruption, and lack of economic diversification, some solutions incorporating tax policy have been advanced.

Firstly, taxation policy needs to be linked to balancing revenues with planned fiscal deficits, and such policies need to be viewed through the prospect of generating sustainable GDP growth and hence, future taxation income for an economy. Thus, a return-on-investment perspective with relevant payback period assumptions needs to be incorporated to ensure that taxes collected are placed in public sector projects with potential economic value generation.

Secondly, tax policies have seen a progression from the use of direct taxes such as trade-related taxes and personal income tax to indirect taxation such as VAT (Value Added Tax), GST (Goods & Services Tax) and other forms of consumer and sales taxes. While it can be argued that such taxes are inequitable and regressive in the sense that it does not tax the rich more relative to the poor, which is of particular importance in emerging economies, it should also be noted that indirect taxes are subject to less manipulation and will be able to reach a larger base of the population. Indirect taxes such as VAT and GST are taxes on the final good and considered "non-discretionary" unlike direct taxes which allow for the presence of corruption at collection points or tax avoidance during the self-assessment procedures. Tax avoidance can come in the form of tax shifting to an international tax haven, excessive use of exemptions or substitution between corporate and personal taxes depending on which is more favourable. While the size of the informal economy is also a common argument against indirect taxes, this is mitigated by the fact that it would at some point be indirectly taxed as it interacts with the formal economy. Apart from these reasons, empirical studies show that the share of global GDP from indirect taxation has increased for both developing and developed economies, which is suggestive of a tendency, if not some collective wisdom that such taxes are probably more effective. Additionally, economies which advance from a resource-based one to one which is services-oriented, would tend to have more traction on indirect taxes.

Ultimately, what the sovereign credit analyst should question to determine the quality of tax policy and its macroeconomic impacts are: i) whether economic composition is largely primary or tertiary, and if indirect taxes were imposed, whether the share of the tertiary economy is sufficient to produce meaningful government revenues; ii) if human and technological infrastructure is sufficient to effect a shift from an archaic tax system to one which has a broad, efficient and effective reach; iii) whether tax revenues collected are being utilised for investments which generate future value for the economy; iv) to gauge if total tax revenues collected are sufficient to fund government expenses; v) whether the regressive nature of an indirect tax considered inequitable to the electorate, and finally, vi) to assess, probably with difficulty, the related costs of potential civil dissent sufficient to warrant a change in the existing tax system.

Essay 16

October 2014

A Bumpy Ride for Emerging Market Bonds

There is often confusion when market reactions do not appear to represent fundamental reality accurately. However, this issue is not one which is given up as unapproachable volatility. A resolution of this would be to understand that if and when fundamentals mirror sentiment, market directionality is enhanced, as opposed to a less directional trading range. As such, the irrational and rational need not be confined in the nebula of philosophy but can be constructively expressed as an executable investing decision. Other issues being considered include the size of the growing credit market and supply of liquidity which has been leveraged by investors, creating arbitrage between real assets and the financial markets. This is thus a classic case of an unhealthy resource transfer between an area of excess to an area of deficit. Also, this is in turn linked to easy monetary policy which has been supportive of the carry trade, with low interest rates and quantitative easing creating this excess.

~

The recent weeks have seen weaker sentiment envelope the Emerging Markets (EM) space. Again, this would lead to worries over whether this is representative of a generalised sell-off, and how protracted this could be. I would believe that the answer is not straightforward, and the markets would evolve along three dimensions:

i) the frequency of volatile trades in the months to come;

ii) the persistence and strength of the carry trade, linked to G3 central bank policy;

iii) event risks especially geopolitics.

Why the volatility?

The first dimension is particularly important in setting the overtone that recent losses in the EM space represent two-way volatility, in that recent events have been event-driven rather than structural. The former scenario is preferable since it represents both risks and opportunities. The first scenario is also characterised by short-term event risks. This can include a shift in market expectations that the central bank would be hawkish rather than dovish, or certain expectations on monetary policy were not met. For example, the recent selling on the Malaysian Ringgit was driven by actual policy not meeting expectations, and in this case, the lack of an interest rate hike. Furthermore, there has been a n upward reversal of US Treasury yields following a dip below 2%, in line with the Federal Reserve's end of US Treasury purchases this month. However, it is difficult to be too much of an EM bear when: i) the end of Treasury purchases was expected and not an outright reversal of Quantitative Easing (QE); and ii) the rise in US Treasury yields represented more of an exit from overvalued US Treasuries rather than a fundamental shift in the global macroeconomic pulse.

Hence, would the market evolve along one-sided risks or is this more of a two-way market? To answer this question, we need to first analyse the extent to which expectations are well balanced.

Will the volatility point to a bull or bear market?

This is important since in market terms, a mono-directional scenario helps mark either a bull or bear market, as opposed to a trading range market where directionality is more limited or more multi-directional. To explain from a behavioural finance viewpoint, a mono-directional market is one in which both fundamentals and expectations pair to accurately represent longer term risks, whereas a multi-directional market is encouraged by discrepancies between reality and expectations. This is because reality and expectations need to be self-reinforcing, without which, it is difficult to support the scenario of a veritable bull or bear market.

Over the last month, it is possible that expectations have not been met, causing volatility, simply because the perceived strength of policy measures were considered too innocuous. In the recent European Central Bank (ECB) meeting, the monetary policy setting remained accommodative, and met expectations that the range of securities purchased by the central bank would broaden and deepen, although disappointed markets on the lack of a specific measurable target. On this, it may not be necessary and fundamentally sound for the ECB to jump the gun and commit to a specific target, and in this case, market fluctuations are responding to hope rather than logical economic outcomes. In fact, the ECB does not have a mandate to over-communicate, since excessively explicit communications and pre-commitments by a central bank may eventually lead to a greater gap between reality and expectations, definitely an unfavourable situation for market volatility. In this scenario, the market simply reacted due to prior expectations, and not so much as a correct judgment of whether the ECB was doing the fundamentally right thing.

Expect a more multi-directional scenario

The fact that markets react to the tensions between hope, fear and reality are suggestive of both opportunities and risks. This encapsulates a more balanced, multi-directional scenario, unlike severe macroeconomic dislocations, which tend to unfold mono-directionally. Hence, we should analyse how we are located within this spectrum of multi-directionality and mono-directionality.

As explained above, some of the recent market reactions are clearly short-term event-driven, eclipsing any clear or pervasive structural trend. Today, the risk of such a structural trend taking shape has yet to solidify, given multi-directional pathways for central bank policy. The US appears to be recovering slowly, while the EU and Japan continue to be mired in poor economic growth prospects and deflation. At the same time, it is difficult to point all fingers at a systemic risk attack occurring in the EM. There are signs of political change in Thailand and Indonesia although these are largely localised in nature. While growth is maintained at current levels leading to economic prosperity, the risks of political events morphing into social unrest appear very distant. Nonetheless, while the Ukraine-Russia tensions appeared to be a very real risk in the EM Europe financial markets space, risks here are beginning to fade. From a more optimistic viewpoint, initial skirmishes would eventually retract to economic interests preventing a full-fledged war. Too much investment and interdependencies are at stake, such as the massive energy pipeline projects between East and West Europe. While polls appear to encourage an initially aggressive stance by protectors of sovereignty, I suppose some initial drama would be preferable to blindly moving into destructive behaviour.

Hence, the fact that the risks have not seen much of a spillover across the whole EM bloc, that is, between EM Europe and EM Asia, there appears to be a dichotomy between multi-directional opportunities. This has held back the materialisation of mono-directional risks in the EM, due to the geographic diversification of risks and the differences between G3 and EM economic prospects.

The carry trade remains supportive

Regarding the carry trade, the analysis continues to be linked to the policies of central banks at the G3 and whether yield differentials continue to support this rational bubble. The bubble is "rational" since the key driver of lower bond yields have been mainly attributed to cheap funding allowing investors to leverage and invest in higher yield securities. Retail investors are increasingly taking on the role of sophisticated fund managers following enlarged, margin-financed portfolios. However, the carry trade-with-leverage model may not be sustainable or produce real economic value. Such investors have a tendency of investing based on yield margins, rather than allocating resources to companies which need it for viable projects. Furthermore, excess credit supply can feed into inflation and a lack of stringent credit evaluation. As a result, the bubble worsens when this "rationality" is benchmarked against the investing style of others in the community. Interestingly and ironically, the problem here is supported by a mismatch between reality and expectations, which also suggests that the worries could materialise in an adverse market scenario when reality matches beliefs, and in this case, when the market collectively believes that we are, in fact, in a bubble scenario.

As long as G3 interest rates remain low, credit supply will continue to find its way to higher yielding securities, and it is quite common that little regard will be given to the concept of fundamentals, which has become increasingly academic in spite of its great value. What we see at work today is the concept of financial markets arbitrage, on the back of a disproportionately large financial market relative to the real asset market. As financial liberalisation continues, financial inflows into the emerging markets will rise, with or without a concomitant improvement in fundamentals or institutional quality. Portfolio flows, by their very nature, are unable to assess the merits and risks of a security as linked to the underlying real asset, simply because of insufficient information and the somewhat "Ivory Tower" nature of investing. It is not possible to clone an analyst or fund manager to monitor individual projects' credit quality and the pulse of the economy on the ground within a country or across nations, which are the basis for the inter-regional carry trade. Financial resource allocation can only do its best and occur on limited information. It is within this limit to knowledge where arbitrage opportunities occur, and where the boom-bust cycle inevitably renews.

Essay 17

November 2014

Commodity Exporters & Emerging Market Risks

At times, market views can turn extreme, and this is where alternative views need to be presented, lest heavy investment allocations and excessive risk are taken on either side of the trade. This essay illustrates the deliberate moderation of an extreme narrative, previously targeted at commodity producers and is a somewhat rhetorical device rather than a personal belief towards a one-sided view. Very often, it is this war of words which help impute information which comprises the consequences of market expectations.

~

Most of my discussions have hardly referred to country specific issues, preferring to focus on a broad range of common issues which affect the fixed income markets and the closely related currency markets. This essay in particular, continues to hold the view that there are common issues which affect the market with similar characteristics, and alludes to Malaysia in some instances at the heart of this case study. This discussion expresses the voice of devil's advocate by: i) challenging popular notions of closely correlated currency weaknesses with the fixed income markets; ii) challenging skewed beliefs toward commodity exporters; and iii) hence, aims to avoid extreme views which could lead to laggard strategies of timing the market.

There is a common perception that a sell-down in the bond markets tend to be accompanied by currency weakness. Traditionally, this would lead to capital outflows and a rise in interest rates or bond yields. There are several explanations for this result. For example, excessively low yields in a market would mean greater returns elsewhere which would cause capital outflows and selling of bonds, to allow for a subsequent upward adjustment in yields. Higher yields elsewhere would also suggest that the currency is insufficiently weak, which means that current-period overvaluation results in a diminishment of future-period returns. However, this has been empirically difficult to prove.

On the first point regarding a weak bond and currency market, we have yet to see a material rise in fixed income yields above recent months' averages despite currency weakness, and in Malaysia's case, it has struggled to rise past 4%. On the ground, we understand many investors have been waiting for this benchmark level of return but to no avail. However, is the weak currency then compensating for insufficiently high yields on the bond market?

To this question, the answer is probably "no". Firstly, the weak currency has to do with the concern that Malaysia, as a petroleum exporter, is affected by low crude oil prices, compounded by declining palm oil prices as well. This would then affect the current account balance. However, this is also partly offset by the decline in petrol subsidies, although this would not be sufficient to stem a lower exports balance. Meanwhile, other commodity exporters such as Indonesia may be misunderstood, since the decline in oil prices would also mean fewer petrol subsidies, and not necessarily be negative for the country. Furthermore, most of these commodity exporters in the region, such as Malaysia, Indonesia, and Australia have been focusing a lot more on domestic expansion and the services sector of the economy, and the trend has been quite encouraging given the growth rates in these segments of the respective economies.

Hence, there is a time-varying aspect to the argument, and without cognisance of these arguments, the risk of laggard investment strategies would follow. As mentioned above, the economic diversity is changing for these commodity exporters. Secondly, currency weakness will be natural and would be supportive of exports at a later stage. Thirdly, there is no incentive for a single currency to outshine all others, and in this case, the US Dollar. Remember that with Quantitative Easing (QE) intact in Europe and Japan, US Dollar strength cannot outperform too excessively; while sustained US Dollar strength is likely to be steadily persistent, a, excessive appreciation may find little support.

As always, criticisms on longer-term issues have often been levelled at commodity producing countries. In discussions with global investors, the "Dutch Disease" and "Middle Income Trap" arguments were brought up amidst recent selling on the Malaysian Ringgit. It is interesting that some of these issues were brought up alongside the recent Ringgit weakness, since some of these arguments are related to the structural nature of commodity exporters. Thus, the endowment theories of economic development are at play; hence, there is no support for this being an incremental risk specific to the current period. Another issue which was brought up was the slow progress on various fiscal spending and infrastructure development programmes. However, I would question whether it is naïve to expect the government bureaucracy to keep up with private sector notions of efficiency. There definitely needs to be a moderation of certain expectations with the issue of execution in developing economies. At least, I gather a very different set of modest expectations from investors on the ground who have been used to these games at developing markets.

Empirically speaking, there is also little support for further severe Ringgit weakness from current levels, although the curve ball would always be a sentiment overshoot. However, we can analyse this where possible, through past experience and fundamentals. Note that the Malaysian Ringgit was trading at roughly 2.95-3.20 from mid-2011 to mid-2013 and has found a new range after mid-2013 at 3.15-3.35 to the present period (some might call this new range a "structural break"). Interestingly, when the Ringgit hit the top end of the first range (mid-2011 to mid-2013) at 3.20 in 2013, economists were mulling the risk of the current account balance potentially reaching zero to negative, but that did not occur; even so, the Ringgit was stronger back then versus today. In fact, the current account balance-to-GDP ratio of Malaysia has stayed firmly above 4% ever since 2011, and this is expected to remain the same going forward into 2015, in the context of our above arguments mitigating concerns over the current account balance for commodity exporters. Supporting a healthy balance of payments position at Malaysia would be the ongoing reduction of the fiscal deficit-to-GDP ratio, suggesting no negative transmission of the public sector deficit to our forecast of a stable current account balance-to-GDP ratio next year.

Hence, is the capital account the real concern? Again, we are sceptical of the argument that the tapering of QE in the US would lead to a massive capital outflow. In fact, QE has ended in October-2014 and maybe that's why we have seen some of the resulting weakness in the Ringgit.

However, the counterargument is that the end of US QE had been discussed and hence is not new news to the market. Additionally, it is probable that insufficient credence has been given regarding the impact of additional stimulus, credit expansion, and low interest rates in Europe and Japan, not to mention additional QE. The deflation and demographics in these major economies continue to warrant a watchful eye, as growth could risk stagnation if policy makers are complacent. Hence, with these economies suffering from poor growth and yields, global growth has yet to improve collectively, providing an important investment case for Emerging Asia.

Essay 18

December 2014

Positioning for a Return of Volatility in 2015

At the end of 2014, the financial markets continue to be concerned over the role of central bank policy, and this has remained a recurrent theme, whether obsessively or not. During this period, discussions over the divergence of monetary policies between the emerging markets and developed markets were part of the global decoupling argument which was popular at that time. In retrospect, there has been a vacillation between decoupling and recoupling arguments and perhaps there is no need to have that clear delineation across markets. These forms of generalisations can be dangerous if country-specific risks are ignored and a psychology of diversification-aversion is developed.

~

The market over the last few years was characterised by a significant degree of homogeneity in central bank and government policies as the developed economies were mired in financial crisis following 2007/08, which saw the G3 central banks collectively enact unorthodox monetary policy. Several years have passed after the Great Financial Crisis, and 2014 began to see a shift in notions of homogeneity seen after 2007/08, particularly in the second half of 2014, as equities, currencies, and commodities were broadly sold down. This recent change in sentiment appears to suggest that 2015 will be a turning point. Otherwise, would 2015 be a repeat of 2014 where bonds continue to prosper as policymakers procrastinate the normalisation of monetary policy?

Central bank policy & Cycle Stage At A Turning Point

2015 will be marked by the divergence in central bank policy. As the US continues its economic recovery, the Federal Reserve will continue to discuss its potential exit strategy for the bonds under its balance sheet. Hence, the end of tapering in October 2014 does not spell the end of further shifts in monetary policy. October 2014 merely marked the end of open-ended bond purchases. Going forward, US monetary policy can be perceived to further tighten across a spectrum, amongst other available tools: i) communications from a dovish to a neutral or hawkish stance; ii) raising interest rates which is widely expected to occur in the second half of 2015; iii) the selling of bonds on the central bank's balance sheet; and iv) less accommodative terms on liquidity access from the private markets to the central bank.

On the other hand, Japan and Europe continued to face the risk of stagflation, and have embarked on additional quantitative easing. Again the degree to which this form of policy accommodation evolves has further to go. Both Japan and Europe have the option to expand the range of eligible securities to which their central banks purchase, be it corporate or government bonds, and this will have knock-on effects on its currency policy, which is decidedly on a mode of weakness. Hence, while global monetary accommodation may decrease on account of the US policy trajectory, Japan and Europe continue to take expansionary efforts on credit supply. Global growth continues to be highly desynchronized.

Even in Asia, we can see obvious heterogeneity in policy and economic pathways. Within the Asian region, divergent themes which create opportunities for a bottom-up investment view include: i) the move to declining growth and disinflation for previously high growth economies; ii) countries which suffer twin deficits mainly due to oil imports and subsidies; and iii) countries with a transitional political situation. Examples of these are explained as follows:

- China's growth has been decelerating, and this is partly in response to internal imbalances and the need to move the economy up the value chain, alongside slowing global trade, culminating in China's recent rate cut and the likelihood of further policy accommodation. China's GDP growth is forecasted at 7% in 2015, declining from 10.4% in 2010. Another major economy, India, is also slowing, with the decline in inflation allowing the central bank latitude in cutting interest rates in 2015; India's GDP growth is expected to decline from 9.4% in 2010 to slightly over 6% in 2015.

- The decline in commodity prices, particularly oil, may benefit heavy oil importers such as India and Indonesia, translating into better fiscal balance and current account balances. The improvement in these metrics should bode well for sentiment which may ameliorate recent concerns over the balance of payments volatility, given the twin deficits of these economies.

- Malaysia and Thailand are two economies with low historical volatility on both the bond and currency markets and would have been considered attractive given the currently weak sentiment and uncertainty. However, these countries face psychological and political risks. Malaysia's currency and bond markets have been reacting adversely to the decline in lower oil prices, even though Malaysia has been a net oil importer for the first eight months of this year while the fiscal deficit has continuously declined to below 4% compared to 5.4% In 2010. Meanwhile, Thailand continues to face uncertainties over the junta's rule and potential advancement to a fully functioning government, given dysfunctional politics. However, we note that these two economies have current account surpluses despite fiscal deficits. South Korea also has a healthy current account balance projected at more than 6% of GDP in 2014, although its traditional currency volatility is further compounded by the market's impression of South Korea as a major exporter, even if its balance of payments position is strong enough to withstand a short-term shock.

- Moving over to the highly rated sovereigns, Singapore and Hong Kong, these economies are expected to have fiscal and current account surpluses with very strong foreign exchange reserves in 2015. However, despite their strong fundamentals, these capital markets are highly open and continue to be affected by market volatility, with a very high correlationship (greater than 80%) to US Treasury yields. Investing in these economies will have to come with the mindset of nimble market risk management with the pricing of the sovereign credit risk component well-taken care of.

Maintain a watchful eye over capricious markets

Following the above comments, fundamentals should not be confused with market volatility, technicals and flows. As we have seen through the recent risk-off moves across the globe, psychological finance and herd behaviour can play a major role in determining investment returns. The question is, have recent moves been more flow or fundamentally driven? This question is important since fundamentally-justified market moves tend to be more durable and impactful.

To address this question, it is observed that the macroeconomic position of Asian markets alongside macroprudential and regulatory credibility remain significantly better than where it was compared to the last two major crises in 1997/98 and 2007/08. Currently, currency regimes are more flexible (as compared to pegged or fixed regimes) which allows quick adjustments to both trade and capital flows, and foreign exchange reserves in Asia are mostly above eight months of imports, while ongoing Basel III implementation is improving the quality of banking systems.

However, sovereign credit metrics and the macroeconomic outlook are only part of the equation in assessing financial markets valuations. With the inflexion point most of the market expects to face in 2015, the flow and fear factor would play a major role in determining the investment view.

A dominant fear factor plaguing the markets is the strengthening US Dollar. Factors pushing the US Dollar higher and EM currencies lower would be the concern of the US tightening monetary policy at an aggressive pace, caused by a faster recovery. Already, there has been a major acceleration in US jobs growth in November at 321,000 against the 2014 average of 241,000. However, this factor may be moderated by the low wage inflation struggling past 2%, while input price inflation would be moderated by the drop in commodity prices, particularly oil, which buys further time for monetary policy tightening. I think the less adverse scenario of delayed policy tightening is more likely to play out given: i) Fed Reserve Chairman Yellen's propensity for dovishness and her focus on labour market indicators supported by the paltry wage inflation; ii) a tepid recovery in Europe and Japan, and decelerating growth in large developing economies including China, India and Indonesia; and iii) an excessively strong dollar versus other reserve currencies is undesired since this could lead to macroeconomic dislocations such as US dollar liquidity shortages, slower global trade, protectionism, and a potential currency war, all of which would face opposition from central banks on a global scale. Already, we can see that the US Treasury market is pricing in a benign policy environment, with the 10-year US Treasury yield reading below 2.10% at the time of writing.

A corollary of low interest rates would be the concerns over asset price inflation, and whether this signals a financial bubble. The upshot of this concern has manifested in worries over high housing prices coupled with a growing household debt in Asia. In Asia, regulatory tightening has seen a decline in housing prices, causing: i) a rise in the affordability of Hong Kong's residential properties in 2014; ii) a gentle decline in Singapore's property prices; while iii) Malaysia's property prices declined from a double-digit percentage gain in 2012 to the current mid-single digit level. In view of this, it is likely that property prices have been quite well-controlled despite the decline in global interest rates and yields in other asset classes. Regarding household debt, part of the concern is one of overleveraging and irresponsible borrowing, and a more sanguine story, is one of greater credit market access, economic rebalancing and greater domestic consumption with an expanding services sector.

Investment Strategy

The above backdrop is by no means a complete and exhaustive outlook for 2015, although it does provide insight for the following summary of strategies:

- Decoupling asset class correlationships suggest the global macro trade is more difficult and bottom-up selectivity is important. The "global macro trade" was more applicable shortly following the 2007/08 financial crisis than it is now.

- Position for the return of volatility: increase risk management buffers, stay short to mid on duration, but nimble on opportunistic trade opportunities given shifting central bank rhetoric.

- Trade on divergent policy paths: bearish on Yen and Euro, bullish US Dollar as a broad overarching theme. Emerging market currencies will face volatility and losses but this should be viewed as a tactical entry opportunity rather than structural avoid.

- In relation to the above, Asia remains a fundamentally sound emerging market: buy on weakness, capitalize on carry and spread opportunities given low funding costs to remain from developed markets; express this via: i) a preference for Crossovers versus outright High Yield and Investment Grade (again, bottom-up analysis is crucial); and ii) overweight balance of payments surplus economies, overweight structural and institutional reform economies.

- Caution on the market of non-Asia EM (Emerging Markets), especially MENA (Middle East & North Africa) and LATAM (Latin America) (true commodity exporters) given the potential reversal of surpluses following the plunge in commodities prices.

- Focus on corporate credits that benefit from lower raw material price inputs, which include cyclical sectors such as transportation, logistics, and defensives such as power producers. The low downgrade and default rate levels in Asia suggest corporate financials are robust which I expect to maintain in 2015. Hence, the overall yield curve and currency calls will play an integral role in generating excess returns, apart from the natural excess spread returns that credits provide.

Essay 19

March 2015

Persistent Uncertainties to Boost Bond Returns

Traditionally, the bond markets are a function of various aspects of risk, such as interest rate, credit, inflation and structural risk. In fact, this representation of bond markets risk has become quite canonical, and a practitioner's lens, offers a different perspective of the narrative-praxis link. Very often, the reaction of capital markets is dependent on a dominant narrative, rather than a narrow representation based on some form of multi-factor model. In this case, oil prices have been rather important to the markets as a proxy for risk and growth.

Additionally, there are differences in which different parts of the bond market react to new information, delineating riskier and less risky, safe haven bonds. These nuances are important since they translate into actual profit and loss results, and an immersion into these tonalities are important to provide a weightier consideration into pertinent ideas beyond the present paradigm.

~

2015 started off with a plethora of unexpected risk factors. With probably a dash of good fortune, I highlighted, last December, the possibility of procrastination in monetary policy normalising with tighter money supply and higher interest rates across the globe. Of course, this was helped by the fiasco in commodity prices. I call this a "fiasco" because just recently, "pundits" were beginning to mull a grand return of the oil price rebound, an impressionistic ideal partly from the sign of a contango in oil price futures despite the ever-present supply mismatches and prescient OPEC communications which can surprise any day. There has also been the exaggerated concern that "all" emerging markets would capitulate when oil prices fall, simply because they are grouped within the "risky assets" space.

The issue with oil prices, however, is unlikely to go away simply (or complicatedly) because there is profit to be made from the extreme volatility that we are now experiencing in the markets. Hence, what has happened recently with the correlated Emerging Markets and Commodities trade seems to have been a function of both propaganda and the historical correlationship of these two concepts in the financial markets. I call these "concepts" since not much has worsened fundamentally. Assuming the numbers are run properly and logically, developing Asia should benefit from the decline in oil prices, since the region is a net oil importer. However, markets tend to respond to the headline news and unfortunately, the potential risks to Russia, parts of the Middle East, and Latin America has been grouped together within the semantically significant but fundamentally garbled idea of the "Emerging Markets".

That said, now that oil prices are being depressed, it may be anyone's guess as to the reasons that could lead to the higher oil prices. A contango conceived by traders perhaps? Or the recovery of the US economy given the slew of positive housing and employment data? A bottom has been reached, opening up new horizons for financial market profitability?

As we can see, much depends on the story of the day, but based on some of the narratives, the coast is not clear. It appears that China is still slowing, based on the January PMI (Purchasing Managers' Index) which read below 50, indicating a contraction, and this was led by pre-emptive measures from the PBoC (People's Bank of China, the central bank) which have eased monetary policy. It is unnecessary to discuss the trite issue of "real" and "quality" growth in China and whether we should trust the numbers since the focus should be on the relative indications and trends, rather than the absolute numbers. India, another major emerging economy, has also shown signs of slowing growth and inflation. However, in this, we need to draw the distinction that slowing inflation is not always a sign that the economy is doing badly, although it does provide better room for monetary policy to manoeuvre. In China's case, the slowing economy is reflected by excess capacity and a decline in demand from trade partners especially Europe. However, in India, the softer inflation was largely due to an improvement in central bank policy credibility and the decline in oil and other input prices. For India, we could suppose that the expected interest rate cuts are more likely a function of ammunition availability rather than a faulty economy in the immediate term, although structural issues such as infrastructure underinvestment need further evolution before presuming the best case scenario. Again, we can see the duality of the story in this, and one should be self-critical in recalling the lyrical "in the long run we are all dead" quote by Keynes, sometimes, if not all the time.

As just described, we can see that the issue of inflation and growth numbers tracking, followed by the decision-making of the central bank of a nation is not simple. Years after the 2007/08 Great Financial Crisis, the worry of a Greek Exit ("Grexit") returns to haunt the world economy, most unfortunately at a time when the EU is facing disinflation and is forced to adopt further "advances in innovative monetary policy". I suspect that a potential rebound in the emerging markets could be fuelled by a displacement of fears and Grexit is an important tail risk or "Black Swan" event which we cannot dismiss. Amid all this noise, the Yen depreciation and the Japan elephant in the room has interestingly been kept in abeyance.

On balance, all these fiascos and risks can only be distilled as further uncertainties and the need for central banks to remain accommodative on monetary policy, inclusive of quantitative easing in Japan and Europe. In a darker scenario, governments would continue to raise debt levels in a bid to boost public sector-led growth, despite the risk of damaging credibility and crowding out the private sector (as if this had not already been done). To conclude, bonds will likely continue to remain resilient as an asset class, as growth, inflation and risk appetite stay structurally lower. While it is true that cycles come and go, a downward level shift of the overarching cycle is highly plausible. If Japan's "lost decade" following its banking crisis has marked a special place in the heart of financial history, I do not see why this cannot occur in the context of both Europe and the US, sharing patterns of financial system similarities and systemic integration. Today, as it is difficult to detect a return to the pre-crisis global economy, typified by the manic-depressive high stakes markets which our predecessors used to experience, bond markets which offer lower risks and lower returns will likely remain much sought after, reinforced by views of today's less confident saver and investor.

Essay 20

April 2015

The Information Context of Sovereign Credit Quality

Sovereign credit quality is sometimes conflated with whether a country is described as "developing" or "developed", and at times, this could be illogically associated with the respective classifications of "high yield" or "junk" and "investment grade" respectively, through their respective countries of origin. As such, criticisms of bias remain levelled at rating agencies, while questions have been raised as to whether some highly rated countries deserve the rating or whether this is a result of inherent credit rating agency bias.

A common theme in this essay is the use of both qualitative and quantitative information and on both aspects, information can be misinterpreted and misleading, even if greater trust is placed on quantitative approaches. That said, even if the fundamentals are correctly understood, what makes an investor's job interesting is the difficulty of linking fundamentals coherently with market behaviour. Sovereign credit ratings thus bring a focal point to information, but it should not be obsessively expected as the best, objective version of reality.

~

The impact of a sovereign rating change has gained increasing limelight following the 2007/08 Great Financial Crisis. The consequences of this awareness are manifold. Positively, there is a sharp realisation that financial crises are not exclusive to emerging markets and developing economies, and that rating agencies will take action to downgrade debt-laden states despite political and economic hegemony. Furthermore, even governments and not just private companies are accountable and answerable to the scourge of excessive debt. Yes, governments can and have defaulted, but unfortunately, unlike corporations, suing a government in hopes of getting your capital back would usually turn out to be a losing battle with marginal returns.

Regardless, the controversy and attention paid to any form of a sovereign downgrade or potential default would obviously be met with flared emotions, and a fine example was the downgrade of the US' long-held AAA rating in August 2011 by Standard & Poor's. This continues to be a stern reminder that the idea of national sovereignty does not preclude a state from market forces or supranational networks of private regulation, both rating agency and media included.

This sets the stage for an enquiry into the importance of sovereign credit quality within the context of financial markets. First, it would be naïve to assume that the downgrade of highly rated economies caught the capital markets completely by surprise, nor should we be sufficiently presumptuous to assume that none were caught by surprise. At the very least, a huge cohort of governments with tenuous public sector positions did little to address an imploding situation in 2007/08, or perhaps, there was very little that could be done.

Despite the blame taken by credit rating agencies, the position of governments' ability to repay public debt need not always have been signalled by credit ratings. There are always signs elsewhere. From a simple perspective, there is the complaining citizen on the lack of a job, or even poverty, and hence the inability to contribute much to the government's tax coffers. Experts have also suggested that we look into the debt repayment culture of a nation, with the habitual defaulting nature of certain South American nations a case in point. Other signs can also be seen from the build-up of asset bubbles, such as soaring stock market valuations or housing prices, for example.

Qualitative approaches aside, the orthodox approach taken by rating agencies is to appraise sovereign credit quality from macroeconomic ratios, such as GDP growth, GDP per capita, inflation, the domestic and external debt position, balance of payments strength, the availability of liquid reserves, and a range of other secondary metrics and qualitative factors. This can be considered the "fundamental" perspective. The "market perspective", meanwhile, analyses factors such as credit default swap prices as well as general market price indicators, whether it is from the commodities, equities or fixed income markets.

As a result, the story of sovereign creditworthiness need not be completely reliant on credit rating agencies. The question is, whether an individual pays attention to the public signals. The credit rating agency is merely the information coordinator, the focal point, and the messenger that those in denial would rather shoot. Conversely, we hardly have an AAA-rated sovereign congratulating a rating agency for its good work.

Apart from the general and commonly understood narrative of linking sovereign credit ratings and political

191

economy volatility, there are also some specifics which I would like to point out, technical details which we might sometimes gloss over.

Firstly, a sovereign credit rating indicates the willingness and ability of a government to repay its debts. I suppose it would be easy to analyse the numbers to evaluate the latter point, although the concept of "willingness" remains a grey area. A state is, well, "sovereign" and very much has the legitimate right to default, even if this is not in its long term interest, particularly in the eyes of the international community.

Secondly, sovereign credit ratings are meant to be "through-the-cycle", although this is difficult on an ex-ante basis. Sovereign rating grades are essentially based on educated guesses and probabilities. In relation to this, the idea of debt sustainability is not a static concept, unlike the factor-based and deterministic process that credit scoring models tend to rely on. In simplistic terms, debt sustainability should be related to the interest rate and its volatility as compared to the GDP growth rate and other indicators which help assess cash flows channelled to public sector finances. Hence, when we discuss expected rates of change and volatility through time, we are enumerating stochastic processes which are not easy to predict.

In fact, in a world where policy interventions and politics play an important role in the economy, the problem of knowledge lies very much in "uncertainty" rather than its measurable form, "risk". The statistics help us evaluate risk, while the presence of human intervention, however sane or insane, only raises the level of unpredictability. Interestingly enough, the markets respond a lot more to central bank rhetoric and news flow nowadays; I blame this partly on the moral hazard of the information age, where information is indeed cheap, easy to come by, poorly vetted, and sensationalist.

Ultimately, it is difficult to assume the worst when a sovereign rating downgrade is at hand, nor is it advisable to stay complacent. There is, quite definitely, something fundamentally wrong from a macroeconomic perspective, but that has not been empirically consistent with higher bond yields or a higher cost of funding. Nonetheless, one market or the other will have to bear the brunt of this cost, for example, higher risks and returns being reflected through the currency market, which then leads to the question of whether it is the domestic or foreign investor who has to bear the cost. Alternatively, if funding costs are repressed through regulation, the public sector through the government bond market may experience a lower cost of funds, while the private sector suffers in the short term, and whether this has a consequent impact on the public sector several years in the long term is again, difficult to assess. I am familiar with the concepts of "crowding out" and Ricardian equivalence, although if one were to delve deeper, there are many criticisms of these theories, such as their Black Box approach, the difficulties of delineating the public from the public sector, the propensity for current debt-funded spending rather than future spending, the impact of inflation and currency depreciation on real debt levels, amongst other criticisms – as usual, it has always been the duty of economists to formulate theories and to subsequently pick them apart. On the other hand, if a sovereign rating upgrade is at hand we could then worry about issues such as a lack of worthwhile investment returns, complacency, a financial bubble, or worse still, assuming macroeconomic stability. In today's world of policy innovation, there is much uncharted territory that needs to be explored.

Essay 21

June 2015

Strategic Coordination in Global Bond Yields

A critique of the canonical approaches towards bond market analysis is continued. In this case, central bank policy is examined, where the input-output approach of policy decision-making could be reframed through a game theoretic analysis where the actions of one central bank are contingent on both the financial markets and the goals of other central banks. It should also be considered as to whether a leader central bank exists, since coordination in interest rate policy is a prerequisite for its success.

~

Assessing the paradigm of bond yield expectations

Often, global bond yields are priced through a fundamentally-determined fashion, assessing inflation rates, growth rates, and sovereign credit quality. Apart from macroeconomic factors, basic considerations further arise out of technical factors, such as the demand-supply gap, liquidity risk, and cyclical herd behaviour. While this approach is valid, investors tend to be concerned with evolving processes, hence the need to supplement a multivariate model with one which considers interactions between market participants. While this may be rather obvious to some readers, we need to at least agree that the paradigm of multi-factor models are highly prevalent, in other words, an effect has to be followed by a cause or causes, although this thought process could be ex-post as opposed to an ex-ante game theoretic approach. To further explain, a game theoretic approach attempts to predict the moves of strategic actors prior to their actions, with the assumed outcome of some benefit to either the individual actor or to the collective of actors. This essay examines this concept in the context of global central banks and makes a case for at least an implicit form of coordination.

Thus, a more interesting approach beyond a static multi-factor model to explain yield movements would be to consider the strategic interactions between markets and the governments involved. Broadening the view of markets beyond trend movements are also particularly important when large financial markets with reserve currency status remain dominant in dictating the risk-free rate, and this in itself should also be seen as a strategic game not just amongst the major markets, but also between the major market leaders and followers.

In the dominant markets of the US Treasuries, German Bunds and Japanese Government Bonds, there is an incentive for the related central banks to coordinate their interest rate or bond yield intentions so as to advance orderly price behaviour, policy effectiveness and maintain currency diplomacy. For this theory to work, it is assumed that central banks can have an impact on market yield movements via conveyed signals. Additionally, it is assumed that collective coordination is preferred over a state of disorder and volatility in the global markets. In practice, we do know that the actions of one central bank have a bearing on another market's yield movements and the subsequent conduct of counterparty central bank communications. In a similar vein, the recent communications by the IMF regarding the need for the US Federal Reserve to raise interest rates later rather than sooner is an example of how a supranational coordinating mechanism for communications is already in place, whether by design or accident.

Capital costs and bond yields as a shared resource requiring coordination

Today, the US Treasury market faces a pivotal moment, although whether the tipping point to this moment is subject to subsequent delays should not be ruled out. Regardless, questions continue to arise as to how much and when should US interest rates rise. In response, we need to remember that a disorderly, sharp, or excessive rise in bond yields would be not only harmful for the US economy, but also detrimental for the Japanese, German and associated EU economies' cost of financing and flexibility in both fiscal consolidation and spending efforts. It should be emphasised that even though lower yields are supportive of lower interest costs and hence helpful to fiscal consolidation, we need to be watchful as to whether this would only lead to further debt-funded expansion programmes – on one hand, this may reflect directly on government spending, but on the other hand there is the risk that this turns up on corporate balance sheets only to become a future burden on government finances and continue a vicious cycle of excessive debt loading through the banking system and credit markets, as was the experience of the 2007/2008 Great Financial Crisis.

Hence, the coordination efforts in interest rates by the major advanced economies remain relevant, particularly in the current situation of divergent growth paths, with the US clearly leading the way in economic growth, while the EU and Japan grapple with tepid prospects, at least in the short term. For example, Greece would have to negotiate another bond repayment on 20th August this year, which may re-ignite further discussions of a Greek exit from the European Union (EU) and spark additional negotiations by other creditors such as the IMF, not to mention the dissent by taxpayers of wealthier EU nations.

A rise in US interest rates and clumsily managed expectations could also lead to a stronger-than-desired US dollar. Again, this is a disadvantageous outcome, since the US is presumably an open market economy which pursues free trade, evidenced by the Obama administration's pursuit of the Trans-Pacific Partnership (TPP) agreement. The disadvantage lies not so much in the prospects of US exports, but the repercussions of negative wealth effects on trading partners through the cost of financing and exchange rate channels. On the former, higher interest rates globally would slow GDP growth and international trade, while on the latter, the world is mutually dependent on the success of emerging economies to develop and contribute to global growth.

A disorderly rise in the rates markets would be detrimental to the purchasing power of the emerging economies, and debilitating to US dollar financing arrangements. Large multinational banks also have significant stakes and a preference for the stability of the US dollar corporate bond and loans market throughout the world, to contain the prospects of rising credit costs should interest rates rise. Not only are banks affected, but also multinational corporations which have an interest in enabling emerging market consumers to sustain spending through an improvement in currency values, and it also follows that wealthy corporations have powerful lobbyists at the major global political centres.

Essay 22

October 2015

The Liquidity Challenge for Bonds

A great part of bond market analysis is linked to macroeconomics; nonetheless, it is important to bring this analysis down a few levels to market microstructure at times. In particular, higher frequency trading today, suggests the need to understand the reasons for bid-ask spreads particularly when executing actual trades on the bond market. The reasons for the liquidity risk premium can range from arbitrary human limitations and the inherent Over-The-Counter ("OTC") nature of the bond market, to more complex ideas such as multi-layered market segmentation. Hence, liquidity issues of the bond market need to be especially considered in fixed income price assessments, as compared to other more liquid markets.

~

Often, liquidity is seen as part and parcel of the risk an investor undertakes in return for a return, or compensation. However, the concept of liquidity is highly nuanced, particularly for bond investors. Unlike the currencies, equities, and commodities markets, the bond market can be highly illiquid in particular segments. In fact, discussing the bond market in terms of "segments", in itself is suggestive of market frictions which could hamper unhindered trading and transaction activity.

From this viewpoint, we could subsequently discuss the issue of liquidity from the perspective of market microstructure. Firstly, the very nature of the bond market being largely an OTC (Over-The-Counter) one would lead to liquidity issues in price discovery. Hence, not all banks would be required to quote bond yields for a particular bond, and when they do, it is usually incentive-linked and not so much because of altruism to do so, for example, the need to "make a market" for a recently issued bond.

The OTC market would also lead to additional market frictions which in turn narrows the potentiality of liquidity. For example, human error, behaviour, psychology, culture and social preferences themselves would play a role in the existence or non-existence of a bond price or yield quote, and could lead to the subjective art of personal preferences playing a role in the quote. In the bond market, each asset can be differentiated by both the seller based on points of information during the negotiation process, and this differentiation can include both the credit quality aspect alongside the human aspect to the pricing process.

To characterise this crudely, it is akin to haggling in a wet market as opposed to having consistently published prices to reduce the haggling process to a bare minimum, and we all know that such negotiation in itself imputes the price of the buyer-seller relationship within. This is not to say that this occurs only in the bond market, but the focus here would be to highlight the importance of subjective negotiation and diplomatic relations in playing a significant role in the bond market, depicting the essence of market microstructure frictions to liquidity owing to the OTC nature of the market.

Naturally, we would then ask, why hasn't the market microstructure evolved? Firstly, the issue of market segmentation would be greater in the corporate bond market rather than the government bond market, given the idiosyncratic credit risks within the former market. Furthermore, corporate bonds are priced off the government bond yield curve, rather than vice versa, and this is, often, due to the lack of a sufficient range of maturities for the pricing of corporate bonds.

While there is a solution to this, for example, financially engineering a price through a theoretical method, market practitioners do not always have the resources or time to do this particularly in the midst of an urgent trade, nor are they predisposed to replace market-based methods of pricing with what would be perceived as a highly debatable, normative, and theoretical pricing model. Furthermore, this becomes even more difficult when we are discussing bonds of an exotic nature, such as those with quarterly or even monthly coupon payments (as opposed to semi-annual coupons), inverse floaters, option-embedded commercial mortgage-backed securities and the like. Hence, the pricing of the bond does not rest on a two-dimensional price-to-fundamental quality axes, but one which is at least three-dimensional particularly since each bond has a different maturity date.

While the issue of liquidity as an operational or microstructure matter seems rather pedestrian, explaining this context is important as a reminder that the concept of undertaking the liquidity premium extends far beyond the more common idea of investment and market liquidity risk, which most investors tend to focus on nowadays given the prevalence of macro-driven news flow.

In fact, macro-driven compensation for liquidity risk as an overriding investment concept could be risky. For example, the lack of a micro focus could potentially lead us to overlook issues such as counterparty risk or structural risks of bonds. Compliance needs, which operate as a risk management check-and-balance, must not be avoided or forgotten.

Liquidity risk issues also arise in other non-macro concerns, for example, surprise regulations from the government, such as the implementation of administrative measures to control capital outflows. The lack of hedging and derivative instruments, or the lack of both supply-and-demand in such instruments, which in essence is also a form of liquidity risk for instruments which should promote more liquid and developed capital markets, are also a concern for investors. Changes in industry regulation could also create liquidity risks, for example, the possibility of substitution effects between rated and non-rated bonds, and banking regulation creating liquidity bottlenecks of lower rated bond holdings in favour of higher-rated bonds. The government encouraging unnecessary credit growth, for example, gearing up on mortgages to support the stock market, such as what we have seen following the recent sharp falls in China's stock market, may in fact serve to galvanise short-term liquidity but also create a backlog of credit risks at a later stage when unwinding of long positions reaches a more earnest level. Bilateral swap lines between central banks, timely cooperative agreements between governments during times of financial crises, despite being administrative planning measures, could spell the difference between survival and Armageddon, as we have recently seen in the narrowly escaped collapse and complete default of the Greek economy.

The story of liquidity risks and judging the level of expected compensation for this, thus, cannot be limited to the conventional obsession with where interest rates are going, the state of the global economy, credit growth, the degree of quantitative easing, and capital flows. I do not expect to have comprehensively answered most of the liquidity risks to be expected from investing, but what I hope to have achieved is to re-angle the definition of liquidity risk and imputation of liquidity risk premiums in our assessment of bond yields, especially important in less liquid segments of this asset class. While seemingly minor, the appreciation of and demand for compensation of market frictions embedded in complex microstructures should not be overlooked for headline-grabbing macro liquidity risks, lest we fail to demand adequate compensation to risks and start accepting ultralow yields as an investment norm.

Essay 23

November 2015

How the Reprieve Rally Could Go Wrong

As the end of 2015 drew near, volatility was a buzzword and would appear to remain so for quite some time to come. Unfortunately, much of this volatility had its origins in the verbal exhortations of the US central bank, however well-meaning intentions might have been.

Furthermore, the waning optimism on emerging markets was seriously considered by the financial markets, partly due to changing growth and wealth dynamics as these economies continue to chart their path towards a more mature phase of growth.

At the same time, it needs to be recognised that there is a great amount of inter-dependent influences between the markets and the central bank, and that the natural jitteriness inherent in financial markets, coupled with policy dilemmas and trade-offs that central banks always face, are inevitable ingredients for volatility and perhaps, the propensity for risk aversion and investments in safe havens.

~

Climbing Out of a Well

The markets have been reacting like manic-depressives, given the rout to emerging market equities, bonds and commodities in August and September, followed by the reprieve rally in October. However, I would prefer to err on the conservative, when the "depressive" part of the equation comes back to haunt the "manic" sentiment which of course, remains psychologically unstable from the perspective of behavioural finance.

213

We need to recall that in the run-up to the reprieve rally, emerging markets had earlier fallen largely due to worries of higher US interest rates. However, the situation remains murky, as US Federal Reserve Chairman Yellen, was unable to raise rates during the last meeting in mid-September, citing concerns over global growth with a focus on the declines seen in China. In the US, the economists at the Federal Reserve noted a softening of economic indicators for the September meeting as compared to the July meeting, while downside risks to GDP have increased. Furthermore, it would be difficult to raise rates as it may undermine the credibility of the Federal Reserve's 2% inflation rate target, since inflation is currently low partly due to the fall in commodity prices. Fed Funds futures reinforced this dovish overtone by pricing in an increased probability of a rate hike to be seen past January 2016, as opposed to initial expectations for a rate hike by the end of 2015.

The equities markets, emerging market currencies and commodities markets have rallied over the last few weeks, taking this as a sign that accommodative monetary policy would be maintained to support growth. Often, such interpretations are well-justified given an ordinary form of interpretation. However, the markets' volatility has increased lately, suggesting that we are at a crossroads or some form of turning point where surprises could be rife.

In this case, we need to be cautious and appreciate the utterances of the devil's advocate.

Giving Credence to Pessimism

Firstly, the sell-down in emerging market assets has not been completely driven by negative sentiment or irrational folly. Structurally, we have to admit that the developing economies have been decumulating savings over the last few years, partly due to credit growth, financial sector advancement, and nation-building efforts. There has also been a shift in the level of balance of payments surpluses, as the exports focus of developing nations move towards a domestic consumption and services sector focus, which is inherently linked to a greater degree of imports. As a result, international reserves had been on a declining trend for most nations in Asia. In order to plug the gap, the capital account has been utilised which is in turn funded by foreign investors, while at the same time, this has led to a dynamic of higher debt levels as developed market investors demand these government bonds or debt on account of better relative carry.

Government balance sheets aside, the decelerating economic cycle globally, and the maturing nature of developing nations, would then lead to a decline in growth. Apart from the cyclicality of the economic cycle, demographics and the population pyramid in countries such as China and South Korea are indicative of an older economy where organic growth is tapering off. Naturally, the massive levels of commodities consumption and fixed asset investments would approach a saturation point, and China is an example which looks towards the future through a rebalancing of the economy towards the higher value-added and services-side of the supply chain. This is not merely a China-centric rebalancing, but also one that we are seeing in other developing economies such as Malaysia and Indonesia. While the growth rates in the Asian economies and emerging markets are undoubtedly high relative to the rest of the world, the engine here, cannot run at its peak levels as was seen a decade ago.

Based on central bank behaviour, particularly the US, also suggests that we are unlikely to see the US growth rate reaching extravagant levels, and it is more likely to chug along in its gradual improvements, while other major economies such as Japan and Europe may continue at their glacial pace of economic growth as deflation remains an overhanging fear. As a result, it is unlikely that the interest rate decision in the US, whether a rate hike or not, would mark a significant turning point in terms of where inflation and global growth levels are going to read over the next couple of years.

During our conversations with the market, we often hear of the common narrative that if the Federal Reserve were to raise rates decisively in September, it would have removed uncertainty in the market. I believe there needs to be a more nuanced reading of rate decisions, although I would have to qualify that I am presenting a deliberately more cautious series of scenario analyses, as is the intention of this short essay to present an alternative to the risk of undue optimism currently being priced in the financial markets.

Firstly, even if the US interest rate was raised in September 2015, the market would still have to face the uncertainty of when the next rate hike would be, since a 25bps (25 basis points) movement in the interest rate is unlikely to have a major impact on the economy while an interest rate signal needs to be protracted beyond a single rate action for it to gain traction and credibility. Further down the road, the next worry would relate to how the US Federal Reserve could potentially unwind its balance sheet which accumulated US Treasuries during quantitative easing. Related to this, is the issue where a rate hike could be interpreted as a signal of confidence, although whether this holds water is dependent on the unfolding of events over time, and whether the erstwhile rate hike would lead to a following loss of confidence given an increased cost of funding eventually. Furthermore, it is difficult to predict if the eventual rise in the cost of funding could be ill-timed and synchronous with a general slowdown in the economy, on both unpredictable factors and the predicted effects of a higher cost of funding.

Secondly, it is particularly interesting to note how the focus on the US has led to a de-emphasis on other major markets such as Japan and Europe, with the latter continuing on a path of dovish rhetoric, adding to the general concerns of ongoing uncertainty due to potential policy mishaps. Easy monetary policy traditionally brings with it the concerns of asset bubble formation, and in a world where capital is internationally mobile, there is the risk that capital from Japan and Europe, with near zero rates and bond yields, is exported to the US. When this occurs, it results in further difficulties in managing monetary policy since excess liquidity from the international markets can destabilise policies, such as rate hikes, which attempt to prevent the formation of asset bubbles and skewed recoveries in sectors such as the housing market.

Finally, if the Federal Reserve did not raise rates as it did during the status quo decision in September, that would still leave market participants worried about the longer term growth outlook, undermining the "removal of uncertainty" argument. In this scenario, there is also the risk that fears of a global growth slowdown would then lead to a rapid reallocation of capital from the emerging markets to safe haven markets, if sovereign credit quality becomes suspect, and worries are amplified by concerns of the currently large foreign holdings of domestic bonds (currently near a third, on average, of the government bond markets' outstanding size in Asia). Several other macroeconomic metrics are also pointing towards this, such as slower growth and deteriorating current account balances, although I would avoid re-elaborating this here, being rather overused reasons. Therefore, part of the answer could lie in the dominant narratives of what investors are thinking, rather than solely on the decision of central banks and governments, hence the need to give credence to the risk of potential pessimism setting in, once again.

July 2016

Epilogue

Contextualised by the critical voice, a common strand of thinking in this collection of essays emphasises a keen awareness of the world as a social construction, no less the financial markets. As with the epigraph borrowed from Hegel at the beginning of this book – *What is rational is real and what is real is rational* – the causality of effects and commonly accepted logic in a social community such as the financial markets remain reflexive, and is a manifestation of ideas, and what we make it be.

This concept of ideas is not the only part of our equation towards a deeper understanding of the financial markets community, but also, the experiential, historical aspect through time. Very often, economic and financial theory is built upon the past, and at the same time that which is being prophesied has a bearing on actors in the financial markets.

Thence, one would wonder about the insights that the telescope of history and experience could have provided thus far. In light of present day capital markets developments, the structural trend of declining fixed income yields and the increasing popularity of negative interest rates raise quite a number of concerns for long-term fund returns and the risks of asset bubbles. On the flip side, little of the potential impact can be known with certainty. An asset bubble is only one when market participants think it is and authorities such as central banks decide to tighten the taps of liquidity. Assuming that high asset prices are not ostracised as traditional economic and financial theory would have us believe, we could very well be entering an epoch of peak materialism, attendant to diminishing marginal returns of the satisfaction of consumerism.

Assuming this holds and continuously unfolds as what is considered as "good", "normal", and "accepted" by intellectuals and policymakers, the pursuit of this cause could potentially set the stage for central banks to being cornered towards accepting the popular and populist view of easy money for everyone. Should this view gain traction, the fate of independent central banking would be at greater stake than it usually was; this is not to accept at face value that central banks have been entirely independent, but to sharpen the awareness that the shape of policies at central banks to come could be very different, in substance if not in form, with stronger electorate-government-central bank links, ushering in an era of political preponderance over economics. This continues to be a perennial debate on the tensions of power between factions in society and concerns that Aristotle and Plato had regarding the tyranny of the majority. Much can be elaborated, but this is beyond the scope of this epilogue, although I hope a greater amount of research and attention will be invested in the nexus of political philosophy, finance and economics in the near future. Optimistically, these champions will discover, conceive and articulate this world landscape to be less detrimental than what traditional economic theory would have told us about financial profligacy. What is detrimental could be a limited view that current capitalist dogma would want us to believe, but that leaves out many ideas and many others in the holistic conception of society.

Parallels to these thoughts can be drawn with the current situation; the faltering solidarity of the EU project and the values it stands for, the decline of the US unipolar power, coupled with the rise of nationalism, populist demagoguery in politics and xenophobic tendencies worldwide. There are no absolutes in canons or prophecies which constitute society, financial markets, and economics, and only what we have created; it is with time can the intrepid human protagonist uncover this winding pathway to progress.